The Changing Face of
Educational Assessment

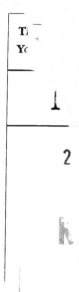

T

Y

1

2

The Changing Face of Educational Assessment

Roger Murphy and Harry Torrance

with contributions from
Diane J. Fairbairn, David Pennycuick and Henry Macintosh

Open University Press
Milton Keynes · Philadelphia

Open University
Celtic Court
22 Ballmoor
Buckingham MK18 1XW
and
1900 Frost Road, Suite 101
Bristol, PA 19007, USA

First Published 1988
Reprinted 1989, 1991

British Library Cataloguing in Publication Data
Murphy, Roger
    The changing face of educational assessment.
    1. Great Britain. Education. Assessment
    I. Title   II. Torrance, Harry   III. Fairbairn,
Diane   IV. Pennycuick, David   V. Macintosh,
H.G. (Henry Gordon), 1929–
379.1'54

    ISBN 0-335-15827-7
    ISBN 0-335-15826-9 Pbk

Library of Congress Cataloging-in-Publication Data
Murphy, Roger.
    The changing face of educational assessment/Roger Murphy and
Harry Torrance.
        p.   cm.
    Bibliography: p.
    Includes indexes.
    1. Educational tests and measurements—Great Britain.
    2. Examinations—Great Britain.   3. High school students—Great
Britain—Rating of.   I. Torrance, Harry.   II. Title.
LB3056.G7M87 1988   371.2'0941   88-1522
ISBN 0-335-15827-7.   ISBN 0-335-15826-9 (pbk)

Typeset by GCS, Leighton Buzzard, Beds.
Printed in Great Britain by J.W. Arrowsmith Ltd., Bristol

Contents

List of Abbreviations

ABRSM	Associated Board of the Royal Schools of Music
AEB	Associated Examining Board
APU	Assessment of Performance Unit
CCCS	Centre for Contemporary Cultural Studies
CEE	Certificate of Extended Education
CGLI	City and Guilds of London Institute
CPVE	Certificate of Pre-Vocational Education
CSE	Certificate of Secondary Education
DES	Department of Education and Science
ETS	Educational Testing Service
FEU	Further Education Curriculum Review and Development Unit
GCE	General Certificate of Education
GCSE	General Certificate of Secondary Education
GOML	Graded Objectives in Modern Languages
GRIST	Grant-Related In-Service Training Programme
HMI	Her Majesty's Inspectorate
ILEA	Inner London Education Authority
INSET	In-Service Education and Training
LEA	Local Education Authority
MSC	Manpower Services Commission
NCVQ	National Council for Vocational Qualifications
NEA	Northern Examining Authority
NPRA	Northern Partnership for Records of Achievement
OCEA	Oxford Certificate of Educational Achievement
PAR	Personal Achievement Record
PPR	Pupils' Personal Record
ROSLA	Raising of the School Leaving Age

RPA	Record of Personal Achievement
RPE	Record of Personal Experience
SCRE	Scottish Council for Research and Education
SEC	Secondary Examinations Council
SED	Scottish Education Department
TVEI	Technical and Vocational Education Initiative
YOP	Youth Opportunities Programme
YTS	Youth Training Scheme

Preface

This book is based on a programme of research on assessment carried out in the Assessment and Evaluation Unit, School of Education, Southampton University. The research has been concerned to document and analyse new approaches to assessment, paying particular regard to the curricular and pedagogic implications of these new approaches and not only, as is traditional in the field of assessment research, their technical credibility. Given our interest in curriculum and teaching methods, and our concern to analyse why change has been taking place as well as exploring its impact on schools, the social and political context of change has been a significant factor in our enquiries. During the writing of the book, and particularly over the summer and autumn of 1987, this context has changed in further significant respects and thus is given considerable attention, particularly in the last chapter when we reflect on what the future holds for assessment.

The book draws on research conducted by the main authors over a number of years, but also includes specific contributions on particular initiatives by individuals who have worked in or been connected with the Assessment and Evaluation Unit. Roger Murphy is a Lecturer in Education and Director of the Unit. He was formerly a Research Officer for the Associated Examining Board. Harry Torrance is a Research Fellow in the Unit and previously conducted research at the Centre for Applied Research in Education, University of East Anglia. Diane Fairbairn was an ESRC-funded research student in the Unit and now works as Equal Opportunities Officer for the Construction Industry Training Board. David Pennycuick was also an ESRC-supported research student in the Unit and now lectures in Education at Sussex University. Henry Macintosh was Secretary of the Southern Regional Examinations Board based in Southampton, and he is now Consultant on Assessment and Accreditation with the TVEI Unit of the Manpower Services Commission. He is also a Visiting Fellow to the Department of Education, Southampton University.

Roger Murphy and Harry Torrance
September 1987

Introduction

Anyone, with even a passing interest in educational assessment in British secondary schools, would accept that currently we are going through what airline pilots refer to as a moderate degree of turbulence. Switching to a more down-to-earth metaphor one could say that an apple cart has been upset. The apple cart, in this instance being a set of assumptions and values that have long been associated with public examinations and which have to a great extent been dominated by the practices of the General Certificate of Education (GCE) examining boards in England and Wales during the last 35 years. History, however, teaches us that the apples can be put back into the cart and it would take a lot of courage (or foolishness) to predict the outcome of the present period of questioning.

Those who participated in the development of the Certificate of Secondary Education (CSE) examinations back in the mid-1960s, or the early discussions about the creation of a 'Common Examination at 16+' from 1970 onwards, will be only too aware of how difficult it is to alter policy and practice radically in relation to educational assessment in British secondary schools. Many of those who supported the CSE enthusiastically, as an examination system that could more adequately serve the needs of teachers and of schools, have largely ended up disappointed by the system as it has developed, regarding it as having been turned into a weak imitation of the GCE examination (Macintosh, 1982). Similarly, those who supported the idea of a comprehensive system of examinations for comprehensive schools in the early 1970s are, on the whole, uninspired by the new General Certificate of Secondary Education (GCSE) examination that is now being introduced (Nuttall, 1984).

If the GCSE is taken to represent the re-stocking of the apple cart with familiar and somewhat battered apples, then some will take heart from the fact that other approaches to educational assessment are being pursued with considerable enthusiasm and ingenuity in many schools and local authorities around the country.

In this book we will be looking at the diversity of assessment practices that are to be found within the profile reporting and graded assessment movements: individual Local Educational Authorities' (LEAs) own Certificates of Educational Achievement, the Department of Education and Science (DES) financed Records of Achievement initiative, and the many variants on the theme of assessment geared to the needs of modularized or unit-based curricula. Alongside some of these other developments GCSE may appear to be rather insignificant both in terms of the curriculum thinking upon which it is based (Macintosh, 1984) and in terms of the extent to which it represents a new direction in educational assessment. Within the other initiatives one can find much more in the way of innovatory approaches to pupil assessment, in many cases involving a much greater degree of teacher involvement in the processes of assessment and a definite attempt to develop genuine alternatives to the pervasive model of external end-of-course examinations that has dogged our educational thinking for so long.

Many of those who would argue that GCSE is already somewhat irrelevant also hold the view, which has been around for some years, that if real changes are to come about in the field of educational assessment in secondary schools, then they will have to be developed from outside of the world of the examination boards. Current developments in the field of profile reporting, records of achievement and graded tests reveal some evidence that this is, indeed, the way in which substantial changes are going to occur. The graded test movement is still in its infancy and, as has been pointed out elsewhere (Harrison, 1982; Pennycuick and Murphy, 1986a, b, 1988), there is still a great deal to be learnt both about how successfully graded tests can be applied across the secondary school curriculum, and about the kind of impact they are likely to have on teaching and learning in schools where they are introduced. At the moment all that can be said is that there are many promising signs, both in terms of evidence for increased pupil motivation when schemes are introduced, and in terms of the way that graded test schemes are so much better placed to meet the growing pressure for criterion referenced standards in educational assessment (Pennycuick and Murphy, 1988).

The idea of profile reporting has been around for a good deal longer than that of graded tests, although the two are often categorized together as representing the major alternatives to public examinations (e.g. Nuttall and Goldstein, 1984). The way in which profiles have appeared to go out of favour and then make a dramatic recovery in terms of the interest in them is a pheno- menon worthy of study in its own right. Such an analysis of the changing fortunes of this new approach to assessment and reporting could be based on the observation that the early Swindon, Evesham and Scottish Council for Research and Educa- tion (SCRE) (and other similar) profiles attracted a good deal of interest but tended to remain fairly isolated pockets of change rather than leading to a substantial take-up throughout the country. Just at the point when one might have expected interest in this new development to die away, that is during the last few years, quite the opposite seems to have happened. This comeback has been manifested most obviously in the many pre-vocational training packages – the Youth Training Scheme (YTS), the Certi- ficate of Pre-Vocational Education (CPVE), the Technical and Vocational Education Initiative (TVEI), etc. – for 16–19 year olds (and more recently for 14–19 year olds), where profiling seems to be assumed to be the major approach to assessment. On top of this have been other central government initiatives such as the Secretary of State's announcement about records of achievement (DES, 1984) which gives every indication that profile reports will be introduced into every secondary school in the country by the end of the 1980s.

Just how far the reservations about profiling that have been expressed by Nuttall and Goldstein (1984) and others can be met remains to be seen, but when any new idea is introduced so quickly and so widely one is bound to wonder about the wisdom of committing so much faith in what still is relatively speaking in terms of widespread operational use, an untried technique. What will certainly be true is that profile reporting will demand a good deal of teachers, many of whom will previously have had little relevant experience of the type of assessment that will be required. Wood (1984), in an article discussing a possible move towards criterion referenced assessment in South Australia, outlines the dilemma:

> Often when a call is made to replace X with Y it is conveniently forgotten that X has usually been the subject of much discussion and reflection over the years, whatever its shortcomings now appear to be, and that Y is untried and unexamined and, quite conceivably, is floated on a tide of euphoric expectation which is quite unrealistic. Sometimes it is better to patch up X and spend more time developing Y. (Wood, 1984, p.2)

Clearly the educational assessment scene in Britain has not

shown signs of much movement for quite a long time, so one is tempted to greet any sign of change with enthusiasm; however, it must also be the case that effective changes should be introduced after an appropriate programme of development work. It is dangerous to claim too much for the new technique before the development work has been completed and decisions about the level of implementation should be delayed as far as possible until the results are known.

In this respect we have been fortunate in so far as the early part of the 1980s has provided a good deal of scope for research and development work in educational assessment. One of the major aims of this book is to draw aspects of that research together and reflect on some of the conclusions that have arisen from it. Thus we wish to look at research and development work carried out on profile reporting and records of achievement, graded tests, and the GCSE examination, and relate these initiatives both to each other and to current, even newer assessment policy initiatives, such as those arising out of the move towards a modular curriculum in secondary schools, and the National Curriculum 5–16 debate.

Perhaps above all we wish to do something to redress the imbalance in previous discussions of educational assessment, which have too often regarded it as a topic that could be considered more or less in isolation from a consideration of the nature and purpose of the school curriculum, by considering it in relation to social and political as well as educational ideologies.

Much of the work reported has been carried out within the Assessment and Evaluation Unit at Southampton University. Within the research carried out in this Unit we have attempted to develop a distinctive, and we think novel approach to research into educational assessment. In essence this has been qualitative rather than purely quantitative, and it has also attended as much to the influence that assessment has on education as it has to the nature of the assessment procedures themselves. This we see as complementing the pre-dominant tradition in educational assessment research in Britain, which, during the last 20 years, has been heavily influenced by ideas borrowed from the field of psychometrics. The shortcomings of this dominant approach in the context of education have been exposed adequately by Wood (1978, 1982), but unfortunately there have been few signs of any real shift in emphasis in the overall pattern of research (Murphy, 1984).

It is perhaps understandable that much of the research conducted by researchers working for examination boards (and they represent a sizeable proportion of all the researchers in Britain working in this field) will have to continue to be directed towards technical psychometric-type enquiries of the existing examinations, because there is bound to be less interest in change in such quarters. Other lines of enquiry that might be advocated will thus require much of those who have more freedom in the type of research that they can carry out. In this context, Broadfoot's (1981) plea for more comparative research on educational assessment would seem to be most timely. The small number of examples that we have of this kind of research (Broadfoot, 1984a; Nuttall, 1983; Pennycuick, 1985) demonstrate its potential for revealing ready-made contexts in other countries to explore many of the developments that currently are being contemplated in Britain. The obvious resource implications for studies of this kind can easily be offset against the problems (and expense) of mounting worthwhile feasibility studies in this country.

The exploration of a wide range of effects of assessment innovations in educational settings also lends itself to research employing the methodologies of ethnography and case study research. Again we have few examples to point to, but the studies of Torrance (1982, 1985) of teachers involved in Mode 3 and CSE teacher assessment have made a start in demonstrating what can be achieved by this type of research, and have provided a basis of experience for the more recent work of Pennycuick (1987) and Fairbairn (1987), who have both contributed to this book in relation to the impact of graded tests and profile reporting on schools, which they have studied.

Having said all of that we would still argue that there is an urgent need for further research in this area of educational change, and the greatest need is for more researchers to leave behind the, perhaps, safer areas of technical psychometric study and embark upon studies which can reveal evidence concerning the wide-ranging implications of current changes in the field of educational assessment. There is no shortage of evidence concerning the shortcomings of public examinations (Mortimore and Mortimore, 1984; Goacher, 1984) or of other conventional approaches to educational assessment such as standardized tests (Levy and Goldstein, 1984); the vacuum at the moment is in what we know about the alternatives. One only has to read an article such as the discussion about pupil profiles as an alternative to conventional examinations by Stevenson (1983) to get a feel for the range of questions and issues that abound. To what extent can research shed light upon these areas in the coming months and years?

In facing the change in educational assessment there are many needs to which suitable research should be able to contribute. The growing level of dissatisfaction with existing methods has led to many people becoming involved in discussions about suitable alternatives. (Even the 'sacred cow' of A-level examinations is currently under review by the Higginson Committee). The overall neglect of alternatives in the large proportion of research work gives such people little research evidence to consider in their discussion. Another major need is already arising out of the increased demands that alternative methods of assessment are making on practising teachers. To move from a system whereby assessment is to a great extent organized by those outside schools, to one which will place this responsibility in the hands of teachers, will necessarily demand a good deal of the training and support systems that are developed. Once again, these topics have not exactly been in the forefront of research up until now, but if the changing face of educational assessment is really going to be faced up to then the time has come for them to appear high up on the agenda of both policy makers and those involved in policy-related research in this area. We hope that this book will provide some impetus and direction to changes that are long overdue but for which far too little groundwork has been completed.

Chapter 1
The Need for Change

1.1 Introduction

It is a central argument of this book that assessment should play a critical part in any educational process. Wherever learning takes place, or it is intended that it should take place, then it is reasonable for the learner, the teacher and other interested parties to be curious about what has happened both in terms of the learning process and in terms of any anticipated or unanticipated outcomes. We would argue that good education, by definition, encompasses good assessment. However we would wish to dissociate ourselves immediately from much of what has gone on previously under the guise of 'good' educational assessment. In many cases assessment, in our view, has hindered the cause of education, and in fact has often been a major stumbling block standing in the way of curriculum innovation, improved teaching methods and changed attitudes among teachers and learners. Assessment has been viewed for far too long as a formal process, which normally involves the administration of formal tests and examinations through procedures that are totally divorced from the educational process and setting to which they are supposed to relate.

We are not alone in wishing to criticize approaches, such as testing, as the only way to carry out assessment, although our position is not as extreme as say Holt (1969), who wrote about the 'tyranny of testing' from a stance of unbridled opposition:

Let me not mince words. Almost all educators feel that testing is a necessary part of education. I wholly disagree – I do not think that testing is necessary, or useful, or even excusable. At best, testing does more harm than good; at worst, it hinders, distorts, and corrupts the learning process. Testers say that testing techniques are being continually improved and can eventually be perfected. Maybe so – but no imaginable improvement in testing would overcome my objections to it. Our chief concern should not be to improve testing, but to find ways to eliminate it. (Holt, 1969, p. 51)

Holt goes unswervingly to the heart of the matter in his own inimical style:

... we teachers say that we test children to find out what they have learned, so that we can better know how to help them to learn more. This is about ninety-five percent untrue. There are two main reasons why we test children: the first is to threaten them into doing what we want done, and the second is to give us a basis for handing out the rewards and penalties on which the educational system – like all coercive systems must operate. The threat of a test makes students do this assignment. The outcome of the test enables us to reward those who seem to do it best. The economy of the school, like that of most societies operates on greed and fear. Tests arouse the fear and satisfy the greed. (Holt, 1969, p. 52)

The crucial role that assessment plays in operationalizing the educational goals of teachers and those others involved in planning and monitoring any educational system is difficult to refute. However, we would see the same argument applying to the ambitions and hopes of the learner – that is if the learner is given good assessment information about his or her progress and successful, and unsuccessful learning strategies, then this will be of assistance, even if in any individual case the desired end may be a different one from that intended by those planning the pro-gramme. Thus to argue that assessment plays a crucial part in successful education does not necessarily close down the discus-sion of what successful education is, or of the role of the learner in retaining responsibilities for his or her learning objectives or strategies.

Clearly some assessment systems go a long way towards defining both educational goals and the route that is to be prescribed for all learners who set off on the road towards those goals. Thus assessment can be seen as the carrot and stick for unwilling donkeys in any setting where one regards the education on offer as being foisted on unwilling learners. Hargreaves (1988) has raised this particular issue in relation to any unquestioning enthusiasm for new assessment initiatives that appear to increase pupil motivation, which may leave aside a critical scrutiny of the type of education experience such initiatives promote:

> What is absent, however, is any discussion of the relationship between the new patterns of assessment and the *content or focus* of the curriculum. There is virtually no discussion within the new assessment initiatives of the social purposes of the curriculum of the essential knowledge and experiences to which all pupils are entitled. The profound implication of this is that in records of achievement, we have a system designed to enhance pupil motivation but without any broadly-based political or professional discussion and agreement about what pupils are being motivated *towards*; about what sorts of things we are committing young people *to*, and whether these have any education or social legitimacy.... Under circumstances such as these, the enhancement of pupil motivation shifts from being an *educational* process of positive disposition to learning worthwhile knowledge; to a *socio-political*, state-managed process of accommodation to the realities of economic crisis, of adjustment to diminishing prospects of employment and economic reward and to an educational experience that, for many pupils, can no longer promise social and economic benefits in adulthood. Motivation that is, becomes transformed from a process of educational encouragement, to a strategy of social crisis management. (Hargreaves, 1988: original emphasis)

The force of Hargreaves' argument, as we see it, is that assessment is not necessarily bad, but every assessment initiative should be viewed with suspicion until it becomes clear what curricular or socio-political aims are embedded within it.

This is a position with which we are entirely in sympathy, and which we discuss more fully in Chapter 2, as we regard it as the most serious deficiency in the assessment literature of the past 40 years or so, where often the discussion has focused entirely upon the technical qualities or deficiencies, of various assessment methods, without paying any attention at all to the much more serious educational questions which subsume them. Certainly reliability, validity and comparability are all important constituents of any assessment procedure, but by themselves they are totally worthless, unless the assessments that are being carried out are supporting and promoting a worthwhile educational process. Thus in this book our emphasis will be as much on the *impact* of assessment on educational processes and experiences, as it will be on the *technical attributes* of recent assessment initiatives.

The change in emphasis in the discussion of educational assessment issues has also been reflected in a change of attitudes towards public examinations – such as CSE, GCE and the recently introduced GCSE, and later in the chapter (Section 1.3) we will look at the development of a growing critique of what has been for many years the dominant approach to educational assessment in British secondary schools.

Central to that analysis is the theme of the stranglehold on the curriculum that the examination boards have held through their published syllabuses. The old adage 'we tend to assess what we can easily assess' provides an apt description of what has traditionally happened within the GCE examination-led system. The plea from the Boards, that their syllabus aims are not intended to encompass all teaching aims, has hardly prevented a narrow concentration on a restricted range of cognitive, academic areas of achievement in both assessment and teaching (Hargreaves, 1982).

This issue of allowing narrow thinking about assessment to lead to a narrow view of educational achievement is critical in any analysis of what has happened in British secondary schools during the last 20 or 30 years. It is probably not surprising that this was the first issue addressed by the Hargreaves Committee in their inquiry into underachievement in Inner London Education Authority (ILEA) secondary schools (ILEA, 1984). They rejected the view that any realistic estimate of overall achievement could be obtained from the results of public examinations. They then went on to outline four separate, but equally important, aspects of achievement only one of which is, in their view, adequately assessed by the current 16+ public examinations. Clearly, their concern to direct attention towards a more holistic view of educational achievement, to include the application of knowledge, social and personal skills, and motivation and commitment, requires a major shift in emphasis. Change would also be needed in terms of the development of new assessment systems so as to ensure that such aspects of achievement are accorded equivalent status. The Hargreaves Committee has attempted to do just this through their proposed system of units and unit credits, which bears many of the characteristics of other modularized curriculum and assessment systems that are being developed simultaneously in other parts of the country.

As soon as one attempts to break away from a traditional view of educational achievement, one is confronted with the need to make a similar break with traditional views of assessment. In the same way that, for years, intelligence tests restricted the view of human intelligence, prominent assessment methods (as used in public examinations) have tended to distort concepts of educational achievement. Indeed, one can go even further in claiming a strong link between the two movements. Much of the development work, in the area of educational assessment, conducted by the public examination boards, has been influenced by psychometric concepts and ideas borrowed directly from the same psychologists who promoted the development of intelligence tests in the early part of this century (Wood, 1982). The traditional presentation of results in the form of single letter (or number) grades, and the aggregation of such grades, by many users, to give an overall estimate of an individual's achievements (and potential), reflects much of the former thinking of psychologists such as Burt and Spearman who believed in a basic (largely inherited) single trait of mental ability that could be used to explain most, if not all, human behaviour (cf. Norton 1979; Torrance 1986a; Vernon 1957).

Many of the developments that we will be considering in this book fall outside that paradigm, and the challenge for those who are centrally involved in changing the face of educational assessment is how far they can go in terms of creating an alternative paradigm that gains widespread professional and public acceptance. The psychometric approach has already been exposed as having major limitations as a basis for thinking about and analysing educational assessments (Wood, 1982) and even major exponents of a basic single measure approach to assessment and evaluation are now calling for a broadening of the enterprise (Tyler, 1986). The Hargreaves Report has provided an added dimension to the new face of educational assessment by questioning a widely held concept of what educational achievement is. They have also introduced a new agenda for educational assessment to cope with, by extending the range of aspects of educational achievement that need to be covered.

At the time of writing we are in the midst of a full-blown national debate which has been fuelled by the National Curriculum proposals, about the nature of the school curriculum. How narrow or broad it should be, and what areas should be core areas or optional areas are key questions in this debate. This dilemma is mirrored in the parallel debate about assessment and testing. The view that assessment should concentrate on basic skills and core areas of the curriculum is widely held. Those that argue for this limited view of the assessment of educational achievement argue that other areas can be taught but are not so important to assess. Those, like the members of the Hargreaves Committee who have argued for assessments that can encompass a much broader notion of achievement, regard a flexible approach as being essential if all areas of a broad curriculum are to be taken seriously and valued, and not squeezed out by the force of demands 'to increase standards' (i.e. through improving scores on narrow achievement tests related to the core areas).

Again and again in this book we will return to the point where we will wish to argue that the debate about whether or not, or how far, to change educational assessment is at the heart of the debate about the nature and purpose of education in schools. Choosing between alternative approaches to assessment usually means choosing between different curriculum emphases, and each assessment method that could be used will undoubtedly have implications for teaching and learning strategies, study skills, and the extent to which pupils need to utilize skills drawn from outside the particular curriculum topic being assessed.

1.2 The various purposes of assessment

Having stated in the previous section that assessment has a critical part to play in any educational process, we would also accept that the role is likely to vary quite a bit between different situations. Macintosh and Hale (1976) have provided a much quoted breakdown of six possible purposes of assessment: (i) diagnosis, (ii) evaluation, (iii) guidance, (iv) grading, (v) selection and (vi) prediction.

This is helpful in pointing to the wide range of functions that educational assessment can perform, although more and more in the current debate one might be inclined to add motivation to their list as a seventh purpose. The desire to increase pupil motivation for learning is widespread, and motivation is in itself probably the most novel part of the Hargreaves Report's four-part definition of educational achievement referred to in the previous section. Leaving that issue aside for the moment, it is instructive to reflect on the extent to which Macintosh and Hale's six purposes of assessment are reflected both in the standard assessment procedures in use in British schools, and in the many new assessment initiatives that are being developed.

David Hargreaves' (1982) position on this issue is instructive. He sees the selection function of assessment as a dominant influence on comprehensive schools, both in terms of the way in which the curriculum is defined and in terms of the images of success and failure that are associated with that curriculum. Thus the Hargreaves Report (ILEA, 1984) seeks to break away from the mould of the narrow academic curriculum geared to the selection requirements of higher education and the needs of a society obsessed with selecting an elite minority through the process of schooling. The main planks upon which their strategy are based are a re-definition of educational achievement, and an entirely new approach to assessing achievement through a school-based assessment of a curriculum based upon units and unit credits. Their analysis of the narrow selection function performed by the academic curriculum is illustrated by a quote from Wilby, the education correspondent of *The Independent*:

> The trouble with our comprehensives is not that their academic standards are too low but that they are too high. Academic standards still have a virtual stranglehold on English education – and they are the enemy of genuine educational standards. Our secondary education is organized to select those few who will go to university and, ultimately, the even tinier minority who will approach the frontiers of theoretical knowledge. For their sake, all our children are being put through an over-blown, over-academic syllabus, in which the dominant experience, for the majority, is one of failure, not of achievement. (Wilby, 1979)

It is clear from this quote that once again our apparently straightforward discussion of the various purposes that assessment can perform has taken us quickly into the political battlefield of the control of the school curriculum, the definition of what kinds of achievement are regarded as superior, and the purposes of school education within a developed industrial society. It is not difficult to find examples around the world of re-enactments of parts of this battle as the 'political-right' have argued with the 'political-left' about the need to focus on 'basic standards' within the teaching of the school curriculum. In many cases this debate has also involved associated proposals to introduce national testing programmes, which concentrate specifically on 'basic skills' in 'core areas'. The National Curriculum debate in Britain is resurrecting many of the same arguments that were rehearsed in the Black Papers, which we shall deal with in a little more detail in Chapter 2, and which have occurred elsewhere, for example in more recent times in Australia and the USA (Atkin, 1979).

Cohen (1987), an Australian with a specialist interest in this topic, provides a useful comparative view of the debate. Throughout the world he argues there is an understandable public interest in reducing education to easily understood and manageable quantitative measures. There is also evidence of such initiatives as, for example, the introduction of national testing programmes, being fuelled by:

> ulterior motives, such as political, maliciously destructive or self-interest, as protection against the success of certain socioeconomic or ethnic groups. (Cohen, 1987)

In a review of fairly similar international developments Cohen, with others' pointed to the successful opposition to such proposals by State Departments of Education in Australia, who became:

> cynical about the purposes of a national testing programme

and the motives of its proponents.... They sought to pre-vent the possibility of invidious comparisons being made between states, government and non-government systems and ethnic groups, a concern shared by the representatives of non-government schools and many interest groups. (Power *et al.* 1982, p. 27)

Cohen (1987) concludes that if one really wants to discuss 'educational standards' in an informed and meaningful way, then it is necessary to clarify first of all what is meant by the term and then prepare oneself for a much more complicated and involved analysis than normally takes place when this topic comes up in brief television debates or in the tabloid headlines:

> The accurate and valid assessment of standards indeed represents a complex professional set of challenges. The seeming precision and accuracy of published quantitative data mask the difficulties of adequately selecting or deter-mining and representing the range of criteria which truly reflect educational standards. (Cohen, 1987)

There is no doubt at all that the public view of assessment in schools has been dominated by both the selection function, referred to by Hargreaves, and the accountability demands, which have been explored by Cohen. Clearly, both of these functions are necessary, and are certainly important enough to warrant im-provements in the often inadequate way in which they are carried out. What is also necessary, however, is the need to ensure that these particular purposes, or functions of educational assessment, are not allowed to dominate both the entire school curriculum and the complete range of assessment procedures that are associated with it.

Unfortunately, in the past selection, along with grading and prediction, have tended to dominate thinking and practice in relation to educational assessment. Lip service is often paid to Macintosh and Hale's (1976) other three purposes of assessment, but in reality diagnosis, evaluation and guidance have a very small part to play in most assessment schemes. This is in spite of the fact that most educationalists acknowledge that these are the more important and educationally beneficial characteristics of the assessment of any particular course or educational experience.

Most traditional assessment systems are organized in such a way that they militate against this type of formative use. The assessment procedures are frequently carried out towards the end of a course or unit of work, are veiled in secrecy, and the results, when they are given to the pupils or students, are usually coded in a language of grades which gives them little constructive insight into the nature of their performance. The idea that a student might diagnose particular learning difficulties from a single letter (or number) grade which covers two or in some cases many more years of study, is in itself laughable. Furthermore, the widespread practice of not returning examination scripts or test papers to students, and not revealing marking procedures, or entering into any kind of post-assessment discussion of the work of individuals, are all features of an approach to assessment which emphasizes the 'rites of entry' selection function and destroys most if not all educational benefits which could be derived from it.

Another major contribution to our thinking about the social as opposed to educational functions performed by most school assessment systems has been made by Broadfoot (1984a). In a very valuable edited collection of papers she and her contributors have cast new light on the power struggle involved in bringing about change in the world of assessment. Their message accords with our own, in that assessment changes are likely to have fairly wide social and educational implications, and may as a result be hard to bring about. If education and educators are resistant to change then the message is that assessment practices may be the hardest part of all to move. Broadfoot puts the public examination system at the heart of the current assessment scene and reflects that:

> Thus it is principally because any change in the examination system implies a restructuring of the power base in society that even minor reforms are hard to achieve. (Broadfoot, 1984a, p. 3)

The fact that public examinations are designed principally to fulfil a selection function is hard to contest – however, attempts have been made over a 20-year period to reform them, so that they support rather than inhibit the broader aims of the British education system. During this time period their role has remained dominant and changes have been small and difficult to achieve. In Section 1.3 we will look at the most recent reform that is being attempted through the new GCSE examination. This will be set in the context of the former GCE and CSE examinations, and then related to the alternative assessment initiatives upon which we will concentrate in much of the rest of the book.

1.3 Various attempts at change – GCSE and the alternatives

Historians of educational assessment, and examinations in particular (e.g. Morris, 1961), tend to trace the origins of such practices back to Imperial China (*c*. Eighth century B.C.), when practical examinations involving horse-riding, archery and other such skills were introduced in order to attempt 'to eliminate nepotism and other unfair practices' (Nuttall, 1975) in relation to entry into state employment. The tensions between the inequalities introduced by assessments and examinations and the inequities which they seek to combat have been with us ever since (Nuttall, 1975; Broadfoot, 1986a).

Examinations as such only came onto the scene in Britain during the mid-nineteenth century but, similarly, the motivation was to provide a basis for a fairer and more effective selection system for higher education and employment, especially the Imperial and domestic Civil Service. Most of the old-established universities were setting their own examinations by the end of that century, and eventually a more uniform system, comprising the School Certificate and a Higher School Certificate, was introduced in 1918. Some years later still, following the Norwood Report (Board of Education, 1943) and the 1944 Education Act, the School Certificate was finally replaced by the General Certificate of Education (GCE) in 1951.

The change from School Certificate to GCE involved some minor changes, for example in the move from a grouped-subject certificate to single-subject examinations. But according to Nuttall (1975) the 'essential philosophy of the system' remained and continued to remain 'virtually unaltered' for another 20 or more years:

> The GCE examination, like the School Certificate before it, was primarily designed to be an examination in academic subjects aimed at pupils in grammar and public schools, in other words, the 'elite' 20 to 30% of children in the age group. (Nuttall, 1975, p. 69)

The viability of GCE to service realistically the needs of all pupils was widely questioned, for example in the Crowther Report in 1959:

> External examinations not only tend to direct attention, and attach value, to the subjects which are examined at the expense of those which are not (and within the examined subjects only to their examinable aspects); they also focus attention on pupils who are examined at the expense of those who are not ... (Crowther Report, 1959).

The irony of the fact that 1965 saw both the introduction of a dual system of examinations, with the CSE being created to extend the target group for public examinations, and the publication of the DES circular 10/65 which laid the foundations for a move away from two major separate types of secondary education towards comprehensive reorganization, has not been lost on those who have charted the history of secondary school assessment developments (e.g. Nuttall, 1984). Throughout the 1950s secondary modern schools had been turning to an increasing range and variety of vocational examination boards to provide some certification and qualification for their pupils. CSE can thus be interpreted as an attempt to rationalize the disparate system of the 1950s rather than an attempt to lay the foundations of a 'comprehensive examination system' for the 1960s and 1970s. Nevertheless, the introduction of CSE did provide an attempt to respond to the criticism of the extremely élitist GCE system contained within the Crowther Report (1959), and the subsequent Beloe Report (1960). Furthermore, CSE did much more than extend the target group for public examinations, as the examinations developed through it

> employed a much wider range of techniques of examining and assessing than had been the norm in GCE and hence brought a wider range of skills and abilities into the net of assessment; in particular, the participation of the candidate's own teacher in the process of assessment became common along the lines of the Norwood Committee's recommendations. This participation was at its greatest in Mode 3 examinations, where the department or even the individual teacher devised the syllabus and scheme of examination and carried out the assessment subject only to moderation by the CSE board. (Nuttall, 1984, p. 165)

Another irony associated with CSE has been the fact that its greatest influence in many ways may have been in challenging and contributing to change in the approaches to assessment used in GCE. The 1960s and early 1970s saw quite a bit of movement with teacher assessment, coursework assessment, projects, and even Mode 3 examinations appearing in GCE schemes of assessment as well as CSE (cf. Torrance 1982). Nevertheless, CSE had hardly appeared on the scene before there were calls for the dual system of examinations to be replaced by a system whereby 'there should be a single examination system at the age of 16+, (Schools Council Governing Council resolution, July 1970). Following a series of feasibility studies for a common system of examining at 16+ during the early 1970s, the Schools Council recommended in a report in 1975 that a common system should be established 'as quickly as possible'.

Thus despite all of the enthusiasm that accompanied the introduction of CSE, the history of the examination has turned out to be less glamorous than some might have anticipated. It took a very long time for CSE grades and certificates to gain credibility, alongside the more well-known currency of GCE, and the dual examination system caused many problems for teachers, parents and pupils as difficult choices had to be made about 'double entry' or splitting groups into those that would follow the various alternative syllabuses. Furthermore, the distinctive approach to assessment that was envisaged did not really blossom in the way that many had hoped. There was a general trend for teacher involvement in CSE assessment to diminish as the years went on and according to a former CSE board secretary, the CSE boards tended to develop into a 'pallid imitation of the GCE boards' (Macintosh, 1985).

The long delays that occurred between the calls in the early 1970s for a single examination system and the eventual introduction in 1988 of the first set of GCSE examinations have been well documented (Nuttall, 1984; Gipps, 1986; Horton, 1986). It has also been noted that when the notion of national criteria (for GCSE) 'emerged from almost nowhere' in the White Paper that arose from the report of the Waddell Committee in October 1978, the nature of the debate took a fairly swift turn towards being much more about the control of the secondary school curriculum than just being about an assessment reform (Nuttall, 1984; Torrance, 1986b; Murphy, 1987a). Thus GCSE involves the merger of the various CSE and GCE boards into five Regional Examining Groups. However, the GCE boards will still survive as separate entities within the groups in order to continue their other activities such as running A-level examinations. All syllabuses and examinations which the groups produce are having to meet detailed general and subject-specific National Criteria which have been approved by the Secretary of State for Education (a chain of command which looks likely to be used even more tightly with regard to the proposed National Curriculum). The National Criteria insist on GCSE examinations including at least an element of teacher involvement in assessment (e.g. coursework or practical work), but as we can see from the long-running and acrimonious debate over resourcing, hard-pressed teachers who have to assess objectives defined and decreed by others are hardly in the best position to take on board the scope for curriculum flexibility and responsiveness which has been one of the major justifications for expanding school-based assessment. Furthermore, all syllabuses and examinations are required to 'differentiate' between candidates, with some subject-specific National Criteria (e.g. Maths and Science) insisting that this be done by pupils sitting separate examination papers leading to the award of different grades – CSE and GCE by another name. The latter part of the GCSE debate has in fact increasingly focused on differentiation, the moves towards achieving differentiation through a variety of different assessment approaches (Gipps 1986, 1987), and what turned out to be an abortive push towards transforming the basis for awarding grades to a system based on grade criteria (Murphy, 1986). The rhetoric of differentiation is that of 'positive assessment', of making sure that pupils should not find assessment a 'dispiriting' experience (Secondary Examinations Council, 1985, p.1). Thus candidates should not be presented with tasks which are 'too difficult' (ibid.). The reality is likely to be a reinventing of the CSE and GCE wheel with all its implications for early selection and curricular tracking (Torrance 1987).

In Chapter 2 we discuss in more detail how the early 1980s saw a rise in political rhetoric about what could be achieved through assessment reforms. The way in which a promised move towards criterion-referencing was used as one of the selling points for GCSE by Sir Keith Joseph, when faced with opposition to this reform (including from his own party's back bench MPs), is a good example of this. Nuttall (1987a) has also recorded similar problems that the Open University team had when commissioned to produce a video to illustrate 'differentiated assessment'. This video was apparently never produced because when the team visited schools with their cameras they were unable to find any good examples with which to 'illustrate the concept' (Nuttall, 1987a, p.379).

The theme of the gap between rhetoric and reality in current assessment developments is one that we will return to in Chapter 6, particularly when we come to look at the assessment proposals contained within the *National Curriculum 5–16 Consultation Document* and the 1988 Education Reform Bill. It is worrying how, despite the sizeable problem encountered within the early GCSE development of operationalizing the concepts of 'criterion-referencing' and 'differentiation', they have been given just as prominent a position within the proposals for a national testing programme for all 7, 11, 14 and 16 year olds, as they were in the GCSE proposals (Murphy, 1987b).

It is of course still early days in terms of completing a full evaluation of the extent to which GCSE has managed to overcome many or indeed any of the major problems which led to its introduction. However, the early evidence is not promising and many authors (Radnor, 1987; Gipps, 1986; Horton, 1986; Murphy, 1988a) have tended to conclude that the compromise that emerged from the protracted period of negotiations over replacing CSE and GCE, has retained many of the disadvantages associated with the former dual system. The danger predicted by Nuttall (1984) that the new system would 'be divisive, bureaucratic, retrogressive and obsolescent' appears to have been fulfilled, and a major factor in contributing to this has been the failure to make any more than a minor adjustment to the structure of examination boards upon which the new and old systems were based. The dominant and prominent influence of the public examination boards in England and Wales has been highlighted by Murphy (1987a) as being one of the most significant features in the failure to bring about more than what in many cases have been superficial changes to the major approaches to pupil assessment in schools. This is a view shared by other analysts of the system including, once again, Macintosh:

> The boards which run the system virtually without exception remain essentially administrative organisations maintaining that they reflect and respond to the curriculum and to not dictate it – curriculum thinking is thus something alien to those who work for them. All boards suffer from progressive arthritis of the procedures and from varying forms of tunnel vision. The boards operate today as they did in 1945 and indeed since their inception. (Macintosh, 1982, pp. 13–14)

Thus we have some of the battle lines around which the moves for assessment reform are being fought. Particularly in Chapters 3–5), we will be looking specifically at three areas of assessment development work – profile reporting, graded tests and modular assessment systems – which have come into being during the time period in which GCSE was being developed, and which now to a greater or lesser extent are seeking to either co-exist with, alter, or challenge GCSE in the form in which it is beginning to emerge. Following the general stance of this book, our analysis of these developments will be focused much more on the interaction between these assessment developments and the curriculum and teaching approaches with which they have been associated than on a purely technical consideration of their psychometric characteristics. However, before turning to look at each of these alternative, but sometimes complementary approaches, we will now consider in more detail in Chapter 2 the social and political context within which they have all occurred.

Chapter 2

The Political and Educational Background to Changes in Assessment

2.1 Introduction

It is clear then, that assessment and certification practices are in a state of considerable flux, not to say confusion, at the present time. Assessment has always played a crucial pivotal role in education, but recently this has become much more explicit, and in a much more politicized way than we have seen for many years. The reasons for the new-found prominence of assessment are many and varied (cf. Hargreaves, 1988), but we argue, however, that such reasons can essentially be categorized in terms of, on the one hand, broader political debates over the role and purpose of education generally and hence the place of assessment within education and, on the other, more specifically educational debates – professional debates – about the impact of assessment on teaching and learning. Of course these two 'constellations' of debate cannot really be separated. All professional debate takes place in a social and historical context and, empirically, individuals can be observed contributing to both the political and the educational arena. Furthermore, the 'political' debate and the 'professional' debate are by no means internally coherent or uniform – there are agreements and disagreements apparent both within and across the debates. Nevertheless, educational discourse concerning assessment and examinations can be characterized as having a 'life of its own' and, as Hamilton (1980) has argued so persuasively, pedagogic change must always be legitimated in educational terms. It does not simply come about because of economic change or political intervention.

In the case of assessment, the common origin and occasional

meeting ground for political and educational debate is the long-running issue of 'standards' and the relation of standards to the curriculum: standards of what, and for what? The word 'standards', and the debates in which it is located, takes us back to the 'Great Debate' on education initiated by the then Prime Minister, Jim Callaghan, in 1976 (cf. DES, 1977), and beyond, to the attacks on the newly emergent comprehensive system by the authors of the 'Black Papers' in the late 1960s and early 1970s (Cox and Dyson 1971; Cox and Boyson 1975). Yet the various debates over 'standards' are not so easily categorizable by political allegiance as might at first appear. For although the current situation clearly arises out of a growing dissatisfaction with what schools do, and the means by which we assess and report what schools do, the precise nature of this dissatisfaction cannot simply be located within one ideological or economic framework. It has been voiced by different groups with different intellectual and material interests in education, and with different definitions of what would count as a 'solution' to the 'problem'.

Thus trade unionists and industrialists have broadly agreed on the need for a much more practical and relevant secondary school curriculum and of course both are well represented at all levels of the Manpower Services Commission, a key agency for curricular intervention at the present time; leading conservative thinkers such as Roger Scruton have been vociferous in their resistance to their own government's policy over GCSE; and opposition parties during the mid-1980s, have been increasingly able to hoist the Conservatives with what until then was their own petard – the quality of educational provision, i.e. standards, in state schools; though it must also be acknowledged that the opposition has been outflanked with regard to policy over what to *do* about standards. In parallel with these social and political arguments, educationalists have been reflecting on the control which the examination system has traditionally exercised over the secondary school curriculum; the determining role of assessment with regard to teaching methods and the relationship of assessment to learning; and the uncertain validity and reliability of results generated by even a narrow and unambitious approach to the problem of measuring educational achievement. The remainder of this chapter will attempt to tease out the details and the implications of these various political and educational debates and place them in relation to the emerging pattern of secondary school assessment – the tip of the political and educational iceberg. It will do so by attending to four key features of the overall discussion: the curriculum, the determining role of examinations, the validity and reliability of examinations, and the role of the teacher in curriculum development and assessment procedures.

2.2 The curriculum

Over the last 20-25 years the secondary school curriculum has
been subject to scrutiny by many different interest groups and
from the full range of political perspectives. This scrutiny can be
further located within the overall debate which has been visited
and re-visited continually within English education – that of the
relative merits and ideal balance of an academic or a practical
approach to the education of young people. That the debate should
be visited yet again in the late 1960s and early 1970s clearly owes a
great deal to the growing comprehensivization of secondary
schooling. At this stage the debate could be characterized as
essentially a professional and even intrinsic one, with philo-
sophers of education and sociologists of education trying to
determine which 'forms of knowledge' ought in an absolute sense
to be included in the school curriculum, and to analyse which
aspects of our modern industrial culture ought to be included in
the curriculum of the 'common' comprehensive school (Hirst and
Peters 1970; Lawton 1975). The debate, then, concerned the
extent to which a core or common curriculum could be distilled
from a combination of epistemological reflection and empirical
enquiry. The points of reference for this debate were, on the one
hand, those aspects of knowledge and the process by which it is
created which could be said to be of enduring value and relevance
and, on the other, those specific skills and capabilities which could
be said to be of vital importance for all young people in a rapidly
changing social and economic environment. Assessment and
certification were not mentioned in this debate but the implication
of a good deal of the discussion about a common curriculum was
that it should be encompassed by a common examination for all
(cf. Lawton, 1975, pp. 99–100). And indeed, as outlined in Chapter
1, proposals for a common examination were beginning to
emanate from curriculum developers and in particular the various
committees of the Schools Council (cf. Nuttall, 1984, for a fuller
account of these developments).

In practice of course, newly-founded comprehensives, often
created out of the merger of grammar and secondary modern
schools, muddled through as best they could. Complex organizational arrangements began to be developed whereby, in effect,
grammar and secondary modern often continued to be accommodated under the one roof – with a judicious use of GCE and CSE in
combination with banding, subject-setting and option choice at
14+ allowing the 'problem' of the common curriculum to be side-
stepped (cf. Ball 1981; Burgess 1984; Evans 1985). Such short-
term and expedient arrangements had their consequences however; consequences which essentially involved growing pupil

disaffection and which flowed from providing the majority of pupils with a 'watered down' grammar school curriculum. These consequences were compounded by the economic crisis of the mid-1970s and the growing spectre of youth unemployment. In turn the public face of the 'philosophical' aspect of the curricular debate became increasingly dominated by the traditionalists of the Black Papers – arguing for a return to selection and the pursuit of separate paths for the academic and the practical.

The 'sociological' part of the argument began to be taken up by industrialists, arguing now, however, not about what all pupils should know *per se*, for their individual personal development and life chances, but what they should know for the sake of being able to make an effective contribution to the economy. Schools came to be charged with being too remote from society: too remote from parents with their claimed high regard for academic excellence, and too remote from industry with its claimed need for a more skilled and reliable workforce. These charges spanned the full range of compulsory schooling and, initially at least, were fuelled as much from the primary sector as the secondary. In particular, the case of the William Tyndale Primary School – the 'William Tyndale affair' – was taken to be symptomatic of the related problems of curricular relevance, standards and accountability (Ellis *et al.*, 1976; Gretton and Jackson, 1976). From such a case, it did not take a great deal of imagination for the traditionalists to take the perceived link between the abolition of selection at age 11, i.e. the abolition of externally-set and -marked tests, and falling standards in primary schools, and apply the same logic to the increasing discussion within the education profession of a single system of examining at 16+ which could well be largely teacher-controlled: perceived, in effect, to be the abolition of selection at 16+ and the placing of even greater curricular control in the hands of the schools themselves. Such was the weight of articulated public concern and the DES's increasing impatience with its lack of influence over schools that Prime Minister Callaghan was compelled to respond with his 'Ruskin Speech' of October 1976 launching the Great Debate (Nuttall 1984; Salter and Tapper 1986).

Now of course one could argue about whether standards were indeed 'falling'. Many would argue that they were not, and the increasing number of examination passes at GCE and CSE being gained by an increasing number of pupils, is often cited as one part of the evidence to justify such a position (Wright, 1977). But the issue of what ought to constitute an appropriate curriculum continued to draw interest from all sides of the political and educational spectrum. Moreover, just as arguments from the 'left' took on board issues of accountability and the need to create a genuinely popular state education system, and hence often parted company with the potentially élitist 'autonomy of the teachers' argument (CCCS, 1981; Jones, 1983; Whitty, 1983), so arguments from the 'right' often did not simply revolve around the reintroduction of selection. Increasingly, economic relevance and parental choice came to be advocated rather than traditional selection for the pursuit of academic excellence. Thus successive innovations in the 1980s (highly visible in interventions like the Technical and Vocational Education Initiative, TVEI – less so but still present in GCSE) have extolled the virtues of economic and vocational relevance in the curriculum, combined with teaching for understanding and the application, rather than recall, of knowledge.

Of course we could be sceptical about the reality of these arguments with regard to *all* pupils. Private, essentially traditional, education is expanding and many LEAs still retain some form of selection. Furthermore, A-levels have until recently remained largely untouched and a good case can be made that tripartism is being reinstituted, particularly with respect to the post-16 sector, given the continuation of A-level, the creation of broad school-based pre-vocational courses such as the Certificate of Pre-vocational Education (CPVE) and the setting up of narrower job-based training through the Youth Training Scheme (YTS) (Ranson, 1984). And yet even universities – the ultimate arbiters of A-level – have not escaped criticisms of élitism and irrelevance to industrial need.

In a sense the jury is still considering the extent to which utilitarian values are intended to apply to all young people and whether a more practice-based curriculum can be educational as well as vocational. Certainly by the beginning of the 1980s many educationalists and industrialists alike were arguing that educational institutions generally, and secondary schools in particular, were narrow and unresponsive: to the needs of the majority of pupils from one point of view, to the needs of industry from the other. Thus the argument over 'standards' had begun to develop into an argument over the appropriateness of educational provision and the variability of educational achievement around the country, with the examination system being seen by various critics as at best a fairly narrow and minimally meaningful guarantor of excellence, at worst a crude and restrictive barrier placed in the way of both pupil achievement and curriculum development.

2.3 The determining role of examinations

Such arguments stemmed in part from employer dissatisfaction with the meaningfulness of grades and titles on certificates, as articulated during the Great Debate, but more largely from within the educational community itself, as attention alighted on the problems of curriculum development in the 1960s and 1970s, and on problems of reliably comparing the results from many different types of examinations. Issues of meaningfulness and comparability will be returned to in the next section but for the moment it is important to explore further the merging of debates about the curriculum and about examinations and, in particular, the claims made for the determining role of examinations in respect of both curriculum content and teaching methods.

These claims about the role of examinations have a long history and can be traced back to debates about the narrowing 'backwash' effects of the 11+ on the primary curriculum and to the general debates about the emerging pattern of secondary schooling outlined in Chapter 1. More specifically, sociological questions about *who* controls the examination system (and by implication therefore the secondary school curriculum) and by what specific mechanisms, have emerged rather more recently. They have been stimulated by educational and sociological reflection on the successes and failures of the curriculum development movement of the 1960s and 1970s, and by a concern to develop the secondary school curriculum to promote and record the achievements of all young people, post-RoSLA (the Raising of the School Leaving Age to 16, in 1974).

Thus curriculum developers, evaluators and teachers involved in new projects identified the examination system as a potential barrier to change and generally felt they had to work within its constraints or be marginalized (Elliott and MacDonald, 1975; Goodson, 1983; MacDonald and Walker, 1976). Sociologists meanwhile began to explore who controlled the examination system and why it should come to be constituted in the way that it was (Young, 1971; Whitty, 1976; Broadfoot, 1979). Initially, such analyses identified the universities as playing a key role through their overall control of the most prestigious secondary examinations, GCE. With hindsight we can see these claims adding to the growing 'weight of evidence', arising from quite distinct sources, about the narrowness and inappropriateness of the secondary school curriculum – the majority of children were said to be 'failing' at an enterprise which was of little relevance to them or to the national economic interest. More recently, however, detailed empirical research in schools and within the examining boards themselves has suggested that the situation is far more complex than at first imagined with such influence as the universities do exercise being mediated through the intentions and actions of examiners, teachers and pupils (cf. Hammersley and Hargreaves, 1983; Broadfoot, 1984a; Torrance, 1984, 1986a). Furthermore, and arising out of the growing understanding of the process of curriculum development, empirical investigations have also explored the active management and manipulation of the examination system in which teachers and examiners have engaged (e.g. Torrance, 1982, 1985).

In parallel with such work some examiners and curriculum developers have advocated that the examination boards could play a far more overt and constructive role in curriculum development: recognizing what some examination boards have until recently always denied – that they do actually influence what schools teach, they do not just examine that which the schools want them to examine – and turning it into a virtue rather than a vice by deliberately framing assessment procedures to promote curriculum change (cf. the case of 'Schools Council 13–16 History' discussed in Macintosh, 1979 and Torrance, 1985). Other researchers have queried the extent to which examinations can be said to be really a determining influence, arguing that pedagogical practice does not vary significantly across examined and unexamined areas of the curriculum (Hammersley and Scarth, 1986).

Whatever is the precise nature of the determining role of examinations – impacting more, perhaps, on the general culture and organization of schooling than directly on specific syllabuses and specific teaching methods (Hargreaves, 1982; Torrance, 1986a) – the crucial point for the discussion here is that various groups wishing to change the secondary curriculum have now come to focus on assessment procedures as a, if not the, key determining mechanism. Initially, such groups could be seen to stand in radical opposition to a traditional single-subject curriculum. Thus, for example, various contributors to Burgess and Adams (1980) argued the case that examinations led to a restricted curriculum and a restricted view of what was worth teaching and learning in secondary school. Thus many worthwhile aspects of education – the capacity to act responsibly, to cooperate, to initiate activities, to problem-solve and so forth – were undervalued as educational goals and as achievements of young people, precisely because they went unassessed. They further argued that the possibility of offering pupils detailed feedback on their progress and of thus contributing to learning went largely unexplored, as schools accepted that a defining characteristic of assessment was that it should be a one-off end-of-course, 'summative' affair, organized to facilitate the social function of selection, rather than the educational function of promoting learning. The way forward, it was claimed, was for schools to monitor progress more closely across a range of activities, discuss this with pupils and report achievements in some form of Profile or Record of Achievement. Such arguments have continued to develop and are attended to more fully in Chapter 3. It is important to recognize, however, that their development has involved not just a series of exhortations to value more fully that which secondary schools already teach, but also a contention that the curriculum and teaching methods must change to make sure that the broader attainments to which a profile would attend are actually achievable:

> Profiling offers the opportunity for teachers to look beyond these constraints [of external examinations] to the whole pupil – to look not only at academic skills, but at practical, social and cross-curricular skills, and at personal qualities. When these areas are included in formal assessment the curriculum will inevitably broaden. It will be necessary to provide opportunities for young people to acquire and demonstrate qualities such as leadership, initiative and perseverance (Hitchcock, 1986, p.147)

More pragmatically, various groups have come together to produce the General and National Criteria for GCSE – subject specialists from schools, further and higher education, administrative and technical personnel from the examination boards, Her Majesty's Inspectorate (HMI) and representatives from the Secondary Examinations Council (SEC). These groups have clearly taken the view that significant curriculum and pedagogical change can be brought about by laying down new parameters for secondary school work within a fairly traditional subject-based model of the curriculum. Thus candidates must be in a position to demonstrate – and hence be given the opportunity in schools to demonstrate – what they 'know, *understand and can do*' (DES, 1985, p.2, our emphasis), although they will continue to do this on a subject-specific basis.

It is interesting to reflect on the extent to which the DES itself actually understands these changes and the mechanisms by which they are being brought about. As acknowledged in Chapter 1, Nuttall (1984) in particular has argued that it is precisely because of the extension of central control over the curriculum which GCSE embodies that the DES suddenly warmed to it in the mid-1980s after 15 years of prevarication (see also Torrance, 1986b). The DES's appreciation of the *mechanism* of change seems clear then. Yet, as we noted above, the Conservative government has attracted criticism from some conservative educationalists over the *content* of proposed changes (*Times Educational Supplement*, 1987). Moreover, as Ranson *et al.* (1986) have pointed out, by making the publication of examination results mandatory (and by proposing to do likewise with the 'bench mark tests' outlined in the National Curriculum document), the Conservatives have enshrined the traditional, single-subject, approach to the secondary curriculum in legislation irrespective of nods by the DES in the direction of integration, relevance, and the production of more holistic records of achievement. Elsewhere in the system the situation seems equally confused. A-level continues at the moment as a specialized preparation for university entrance, though it is coming under review by the Higginson Committee and attempts are being made to launch the broader, but still single-subject A/S level. Also, CPVE has been launched as the integrated, vocationally-oriented successor to the single-subject Certificate of Extended Education (CEE). However, irrespective of the particular sense – or lack of it – which particular initiatives make, the general point to note is that curriculum developers and government alike have clearly identified the determining role which assessment systems can play in inhibiting or promoting educational change so that we are now faced with a series of assessment-led curriculum develop-ments. The effectiveness of too mechanistic a view of curriculum manipulation – assuming that if you change the assessment you inevitably change the teaching – is, of course, wide open to question (Gipps, 1986; Horton 1986) and is an issue which is taken up in other chapters. For the moment we will continue to sketch in the background to the current situation.

2.4 The validity, reliability and comparability of examination results

As we have seen in Chapter 1, debates over the validity and reliability of examination results have a long history in education. They can be clearly identified in the 1930s when the first major assaults on the unreliability of traditional essay-type questions came to public attention in tandem with arguments promoting a more 'objective' approach to testing and examining (Hartog and Rhodes, 1935; Valentine, 1932). They emerged subsequently in the 1950s with regard to the reliability of the 11+ as a selection mechanism (cf. Yates and Pidgeon, 1957) and again in the 1960s and 1970s when attempts were made to establish the compara-bility of CSE and GCE (e.g. Nuttall, 1971; Wilmott and Nuttall, 1975). Such debates received a renewed political boost with the increasingly acrimonious exchanges which surfaced in the 1970s and 1980s over the comparative performance of selective and comprehensive schools, and a further technical boost with the setting up of the Assessment of Performance Unit (APU).

Debates over the validity and reliability of test and examination results have generally been pretty arcane and technical affairs, with their substance being test theory and test development itself: what makes a 'good' test? The answer to such a question would be framed in terms of the length of the test, the number of questions (items) included in it, the appropriateness (validity) of the sample of the syllabus tested by the items, the agreement between markers as to what constitutes a correct answer, the capacity of the test to discriminate between candidates, and so forth; and all this in the cause of the fairness of the assessment to each individual candidate. More recently, however, attention has been turned to the systemic purpose of assessment: the role which test and/or examination *results* might play in evaluating schools and the education system generally. This changing focus of debate has brought to the fore issues of the comparability of syllabuses and grades awarded across subjects and candidates, and over time. Such issues have always been important with regard to the fairness of results to individual candidates, but the current emphasis on them has much more to do with the way individual results can be aggregated and compared. The contributory factors to such a change of focus are many and varied, but once again can be located within, and related to, the debate about comprehensive provision in general, the relevance and fairness of a certain model of the secondary school curriculum and certification in particular. Thus at the same time as 'technical' studies of the validity, reliability and comparability of CSE were being produced, questions were being asked about the relevance and appropriateness of relating their 'standard' to that of GCE, about the falling standard of work which it was claimed was generally being produced in the new comprehensives (be it GCE or CSE) and about whether more specifically-designed 'snapshots' did not need to be taken of the system as a whole (resulting in the setting up of the APU). Thus, the 'technical' debate within the examining community began to focus on the methodology of comparative analysis and resulted in considerable doubt being cast on the feasibility of accurately comparing grades across boards, across subjects and across time as syllabuses and teaching methods changed (cf. Goldstein and Blinkhorn, 1977; Goldstein, 1986; Nuttall, 1986a).

In tandem with these debates, though still distinct from them, the 'employers side' in the Great Debate were pointing to the proliferation of syllabuses, titles and grades which occurred during the 1970s and complaining from their perspective that a particular grade in a particular 'subject' carried very little meaning indeed – what does a '2' in English, or '3' in Environmental Science really mean? What does it convey about what a pupil has learned and 'can do'? This was a theme which the DES and HMI took up as they voiced concern about educational provision and standards of achievement varying from region to region and school to school in documents such as *Aspects of Secondary Education* and *The School Curriculum* (DES, 1979, 1981). Thus the links were made between debates about the comparability of examination results, the meaning conveyed by examination results, the variability of provision and achievement, and the need for some form of national curriculum – albeit couched in the language of 'entitlement' (that to which all pupils are 'entitled') which was derived by HMI from the common curriculum debate outlined earlier.

The implications for reform which flow from this interrelated critique of assessment practice and curricular provision could involve schools and examination boards describing more fully what it is they are trying to accomplish and likewise what pupils have actually achieved. This could take us in the direction of some sort of holistic record of achievement as outlined earlier. Interestingly enough, even the examination boards and test developers have begun to move in this direction, arguing that educational measurement must free itself from its psychometric past and attend more fully to measuring and reporting a variety of educational achievements for a variety of educational and social purposes, rather than simply reporting overall, aggregated levels of attainment (cf. Wood, 1986; Tyler, 1986). However, the corollary of such a flexible and responsive approach to social and educational need is that issues of variable provision, and what some would call 'national priorities' may not entirely be attended to. Thus a second and much more managerially-oriented implication is not simply for schools and/or test developers to *describe* what it is pupils do and achieve, but for others to *prescribe* what it is they *should* do and achieve. The movement is thus complete, from a debate about what the 'producers' of education should provide, via a debate about what 'consumers' are entitled to expect, to a prescription of what the economy (as interpreted by the state bureaucracy) needs. This, of course, is the path which has been increasingly followed in the 1980s as the DES, in its search for curricular prescription and control, has discovered and utilized the hitherto little explored assessment practice of criterion-referencing.

Criterion-referenced testing has quite a long history in the United States where its use has been related to teaching-by-objectives and to the evaluation of new educational programmes. Briefly stated, the educational theory proposes that pupils will learn more when the objectives of a course are clearly stated and when they can receive remedial or extensional instruction at appropriate times during a course (a proposition which has also influenced the profiling movement). The nature and extent of additional instruction would be decided by using diagnostic (criterion-referenced) tests. 'Mastery' of the course's objectives would be determined in the same way and, in principle, all pupils could attain mastery, i.e. pass the course, provided they demonstrate that they have met the criteria by which mastery is defined.

Broader curriculum and evaluation theory further argues that the results from such tests can also be used to evaluate the effectiveness of a course overall and, by implication, the effectiveness of the teaching on it, since the tests should reveal not where the pupil stands relative to his or her peers, but what they have actually learned. Thus criterion-referenced tests would be set and marked according to the stated objectives of a course and the criteria by which those objectives can be said to have been met. If properly designed and conducted, the claim is that they would provide information about what pupils have (or have not) achieved in a particular 'domain' or field of study.

This is not the appropriate place to rehearse all the many arguments for and against criterion-referencing and teaching-by-objectives. Some will be attended to in Chapter 4, when graded test schemes are discussed. Suffice it to say that many critical and even scathing reviews are available (Stake, 1967; Stenhouse, 1975; Hamilton *et al.*, 1977; Pilliner, 1979). The main point here is to demonstrate that a coherent educational theory and technology, based on the prescription of objectives and criteria, had long awaited political discovery in the UK. It had in fact already established a 'beach head' (MacDonald, 1979) in the 1970s, especially through the vocabulary of 'aims and objectives' being insisted on by examination boards when teachers wished to develop their own Mode III examination courses (Torrance, 1982). The irony of the current situation is that the developers of graded test schemes and of the national criteria for GCSE (often teachers and examiners who already had some experience of the use of objectives and criteria, and no doubt acting in good faith) have not only looked back to and built on the largely autonomous professional discussion and curriculum development of the 1970s, but also, in so doing, have contributed to the growing discourse of objectives, management, appraisal, benchmarks and prescription so redolent of the late 1980s. And it is to the role of the teacher in current debates over curriculum and assessment that we will now turn.

2.5 The role of the teacher in new forms of assessment

It was noted earlier that moves in the mid-1970s towards a common comprehensive examination system, possibly involving a considerable extension of teacher-control over the curriculum, were resisted by government. Reviews of subsequent developments up to the early 1980s – perhaps better described as prevarications – highlight hostility to Mode III examining in the context of concerns over teacher accountability as a central issue in debates which seemed likely to render teacher involvement in examining obsolete (Nuttall, 1984; Bowe and Whitty, 1984). Why then have 'centre-assessed components' – the assessment by teachers of coursework, practical work and so forth – become an important feature of GCSE? Why have developments in profiling – inevitably involving teachers even more fully in assessment processes – been encouraged through the funding of pilot projects (DES, 1984)?

Such an apparent change of heart by the DES could be seen to be attending to the issues of curricular breadth and relevance discussed above. Ironically, many Mode III courses had actually been developed in response to local need and in the context of local resources – for example, local sites of historical, geographical or scientific/industrial/commercial interest. They also tended to involve pupils in more practical work than traditional, Mode I, one-off final paper examinations (Torrance, 1982). Likewise, profiling attends to the perceived need for reporting more fully and meaningfully on what pupils have achieved. These are precisely the issues which featured in the Great Debate. The dilemma which the DES faced was how to secure desirable curricular and pedagogic change without simply handing over curriculum control to teachers and to the vagaries of local provision. National Criteria were the chosen instrument for securing change while greatly increasing central control. As outlined in Chapter 1, these criteria lay down parameters for the development of new syllabuses and insisted upon a variety of assessment objectives – the assessment of practical skills for example – which in turn would have an impact on assessment techniques and teaching methods.

This utilization of the examination system to secure change has also been set in the context of, and in many respects been justified by, debates over the validity and reliability of examinations with regard to the issue of 'fitness for purpose' and debates over the promotion of learning by the positive use of assessment processes. Thus the DES wishes examinations to assess what children 'know, understand and can do' (DES, 1985, p. 2) given certain subject-specific prescriptions of curricular objectives. Attention to the issue of 'fitness for purpose' draws teachers into the assessment process, since they are likely to be in the best position to test understanding and application, to test in examining parlance 'aspects of attainment which may not easily or adequately be tested by [final] papers' (SEC, 1985, p. 2). (Some would argue that teachers are in the best position to test *all* the objectives of a particular course, but this is a separate argument.) Attention to issues of learning draws teachers still further into the process since clearly, once again, they are in the best position to give pupils formative feedback and highlight strengths and weaknesses (SEC, 1985, pp. 4–5).

So the involvement of teachers in the assessment of pupils is expanding, contrary to the speculation of only a few years ago, and it is being justified in a variety of ways. But this expansion is taking place in a particular context and under tightly-controlled regulatory mechanisms. The involvement of teachers in school-based *assessment per se* – marking work under instructions from examiners who in turn are ultimately operating under prescriptions from government – is clearly not the same thing as teacher involvement in school-based *examining* – the *design* and assessment of courses within the school. It may be that teachers will be increasingly placed in the position of unwilling conscripts, marking coursework against objectives and criteria defined and determined by others, and even being held accountable on the same basis and in the same terms – 'there are your objectives, now meet them or else'.

Nevertheless, Mode III is still an option that is permitted by the National Criteria, and some schemes have already been successfully developed, particularly where groups of teachers have worked together in response to what they perceive as an inadequate Mode I syllabus offered by their regional examining group. If GCSE 'phase 2 and phase 3' training have had any impact, it is probably through bringing disgruntled teachers together and creating networks for the development of new ideas! Similarly, profiles or records of achievement could provide a mechanism for teacher involvement in the design as well as the assessment of programmes of work. More generally, the increasing involvement of teachers in assessment, albeit highly controlled in the first instance, must inevitably draw teachers into debates over the nature and appropriateness of particular educational objectives, the criteria by which they might be said to have been met, and the teaching programmes which can be designed to achieve them. It is the purpose of the remainder of this book to take this state of affairs as both a theme to be explored and a challenge to be met. The development of GCSE has already been well attended to in Chapter 1. Subsequent chapters, through analyses of the development and impact of profiles, graded tests and modular assessment, will further explore the role of teacher involvement in assessment, in relation to curriculum development and the promotion of learning. The final chapter will draw together the implications of current developments and what we know of them for the future, and in particular will provide an opportunity for further discussion of the most recent proposals to emerge through the National Curriculum consultation papers.

Chapter 3

Pupil Profiling: New Approaches to Recording and Reporting Achievement[1]

Diane J. Fairbairn

3.1 Introduction

'Profile' and 'record of achievement' are generic names which refer to a loose grouping of methods of recording and reporting pupil and student achievement in schools and colleges. Within this grouping a variety of types exists, ranging from straightforward, not to say simplistic, skills checklists originating from and used within individual schools, to complex 'brand name' packages available for sale from examining boards and marketed nationally. A broad definition of a profile or a record of achievement (the two terms are used interchangeably) would be that it is a method of presenting information on a student's achievements, abilities, skills, experiences and qualities from a range of assessments, and often from a range of assessors including the students themselves. The assessment information can be provided in a variety of ways, e.g. in the form of grades, marks, percentages, comments and performance descriptors or criteria. Some profiles serve a formative purpose and are used by teachers and students in the processes of teaching and learning within an institution; some serve more of a summative purpose, acting as end-of-course, or school/college leaving statements of achievement for use by selectors for further education, training or employment. Many attempt to combine these two functions.

A strong feature of the contemporary context in which profile

[1]Some sections of this chapter, particularly Section 3.4.2, were jointly written with Harry Torrance.

developments have been nurtured is dissatisfaction with schooling and with the public examining associated with it. Criticisms have been levelled at the secondary school curriculum for being narrow and irrelevant to the present needs of young people and employers and there has been a growing demand for state education to both account for the resources it consumes and demonstrate a better return on the investments made in it.

Certain claims made for profiling schemes suggest that the assessment, recording and reporting approaches they use will contribute both to solving these educational problems and satisfying these political demands. For example, profiles have been variously claimed to provide:

1 An holistic and individual assessment of a student which takes account of all aspects of the student's unique educational experience covering cognitive, practical and affective elements.
2 Formative use of assessment information to motivate and guide all students in their learning.
3 The opportunity to involve the student in self-assessment and in the discussion of their assessment with teachers, thus likewise to increase student motivation to learn and to achieve.
4 A detailed record of achievement in terms of the student's abilities, skills, experiences and qualities as a leaving certificate documenting what students have done and can do.

These claims for profiling, along with the issues which they raise, are already becoming well documented (cf. Broadfoot, 1986b; Bridges *et al.*, 1986). This chapter will attempt to be rather more empirically and substantively focused. First, it will provide a descriptive history of the main developments in profiling, highlighting some of the issues as they arose. Secondly, it will outline and briefly comment upon the proposals made in the DES policy statement on records of achievement (DES, 1984 and 1987a). Thirdly, it will draw on the author's research into profiles development in secondary schools to illustrate how these proposals translate into practice. The chapter will conclude by reviewing the conditions which the research evidence suggests will both facilitate and sustain profiling in secondary schools.

3.2 The historical context

3.2.1 The background to developments in profiling

Many of the ideas which underpin current profiling systems have made previous appearances in debates about examining, the secondary school curriculum and the vocational preparation of school/college leavers. As early as 1911 the report of the Consultative Committee of the English Board of Education on the effects of examinations on pupils and teachers commented on their detrimental effects. Later, in 1938, the Spens Committee commented '...despite all safeguards, the school certificate examination... now dominates the work of the schools, controlling both the framework and the content of the curriculum' (Spens Report, 1938, p. 5). This concern, over the school certificate's cramping effect on pupils, teachers and the curriculum, was reiterated by the Norwood Committee which reported in 1943. The examination was said to be failing to tap the enterprise and resourcefulness of teachers and, in addition, it was failing to provide an informative leaving document. The report was making the argument for internal examining over which teachers would have greater control. However, it also made an interesting proposal for a reformed school leaving certificate. The suggestion was for:

> ...a new form of school certificate, falling into two parts. The first part would contain a record of the share which the pupil had taken in the general life of the school, games, societies and the like. It would, in short, give the reader some idea of the way in which he had used the opportunities offered to him by his education, using the term in its widest sense. The second part would contain the record of the pupil's achievement in the examination taken at the end of the Main School course. (Board of Education, 1943, p. 48)

It was felt important to reflect not only a broad range of achievement, conveying both academic and non-academic success (it is interesting to note that the academic record comes second in the proposed new certificate), but also the pupil's individual experience of the opportunities on offer.

Concerns about the rigidity and narrowness of an examination-dominated curriculum have continued to be expressed (Burgess and Adams, 1980; Broadfoot, 1984b), but a further factor that helps to explain the importance attached to providing a broader system of assessment and certification has been concern over the 'wastage' of the unrealized talent of many secondary school pupils. Large numbers of pupils have left school with few or no qualifications and, therefore, with little visible evidence of achievement after 10 (and later, 11) years of schooling. In 1963, the Newsom Report on 'average' and 'below average' pupils pointed out that such wastage could not be afforded. The report suggested that pupils should stay on longer at school and that school's should provide education in such a way that it is more acceptable to pupils by relating it more directly to adult life by taking account of vocational interests. One of the intentions of the comprehensivization of secondary schooling was that all pupils would be helped to achieve their full potential regardless of social background, gender or aptitude and in the academic year of 1972–3 the school leaving age was raised to 16. Despite this, many young people still left school at the minimum age without any qualifications. Thus by the late 1970s schools were being criticized both for failing to provide an education which was relevant to all pupils and to encourage achievement in all pupils.

During this period there was growing political anxiety about the country's economic performance. One of the scapegoats was education which was perceived to be failing pupils, parents, employers and, indeed, the nation as a whole. It was against this background that in October 1976 James Callaghan launched the 'Great Debate' in his Ruskin College speech. A theme from that speech which influenced the ensuing debate was the preparation of young people for working life. There were concerns about schools not equipping young people with the knowledge, skills and qualities necessary for their role in society as working adults. Much activity followed in post-16 education where the development of industrially-relevant skills and competencies was promoted.

In parallel with these more general educational and social debates there has been a longstanding discussion over public examining which has produced repeated suggestions for change in assessment, recording, reporting and certification. Concerns about underachievement and the wastage of ability have encouraged the exploration of ways in which a broader range of achievements can be both promoted and rewarded. The recent (though not novel) call for education to have economic utility and industrial relevance has influenced educational values, curriculum content and, as a consequence, the definition of achievement. Assessment and certification are being expected to develop in order to accommodate expanding conceptions of achievement, even, some would argue, to lead them.

3.2.2 *The emergence of profiling:*

A chronology of the main developments

The developments in schools and those in further education are described separately in this section to facilitate clarity of exposition. Also schools are given considerably more space than further education for the purposes of this particular book. In practice, however, the evolution of profiling in the two sectors has not been separate. Developments in schools in the early 1970s influenced the work in further education in the late 1970s. Likewise, profiling models popularized in further education in the early 1980s have subsequently been adapted by schools for their own use.

(a) Schools

Over 40 years elapsed before the suggestion for a more comprehensive and detailed leaving certificate, made by the Norwood
Committee, was actually taken up at the level of government
policy. However, a working party appointed by the Secretary of
State for Scotland in 1967 was given a remit '... to examine in the
light of modern development the requirements for recording
pupils' progress in primary and secondary departments and to
make recommendations' (Scottish Education Department, 1969,
para. 1, p. 5). The Working Party reached two early conclusions:
(1) that the staffing levels in Scottish schools were not sufficient
to cope with '...sophisticated and elaborate techniques for
recording and processing records of individual pupils' (para. 5,
p. 5); and (2) that the variety of forms of organization and
curricula in secondary schools...would make it very difficult to
draw up any standard form of educational record for secondary
school pupils' (para. 5, p. 5). They recommended that no form of
record should be prescribed by regulations not only because of
school diversity but also because they feared such a move would
'...inhibit experiment and development' (para. 14, p. 10). They
did, however, suggest possible record formats for primary schools
and for the first two years of secondary schools. The formats
included checklists for teachers to record pupils' 'Emotional and
Social Development', 'Home Environment', and for their attainment and progress in subjects studied. There was a section for the
headteacher's remarks, sections for test results to be recorded, a
section for the pupil's health record and, on the secondary school
progress record, a section for the pupil's extra-curricular activities
and interests.

The Working Party showed considerable awareness of many of
the issues associated with recording and reporting achievement.
They were aware of the resource implications, the issues of
privacy and confidentiality, the subjectivity of teachers' judgements (particularly concerning pupils' personal qualities), the
drawbacks of imposing standard formats, the importance of using
assessment formatively to help pupils and the need for records to
have practical value to justify the time taken to compile them.
Likewise, they were aware of the need to limit the scope of
assessment not only for practical reasons but also for ethical
reasons. At the time, the sphere of influence of the Working
Party's wisdom does not appear to have been very wide. A point
which is pertinent to the history of profiles development is that,
frequently, knowledge gained by one working party, school or
individual has not been dispersed very widely to inform others and
to prevent both a duplication of effort and a repetition of mistakes.

In England, around this time, pupil personal recording was

getting off the ground. The Record of Personal Achievement (RPA) was launched by Swindon Borough Education Authority in 1969. Its original purpose was to '... provide information about non-examination pupils and at the same time give these pupils the sort of motivation they would otherwise have lacked' (Swales, 1979, p. 5). The scheme was developed to meet the needs of pupils who would have to stay on at school a further year when the school leaving age was raised. Eventually, its value for all pupils became apparent and for some pupils it supplemented their examination certificates. The RPA was designed to help the development of pupils' personal qualities. It was hoped that it would provide an organizing principle for pupils' work, a source of motivation and a leaving qualification. However, the RPA was not seen as a record of assessment and, as such, it was not seen as a system of profiling. Pupils' personal recording is a non-competitive, non-judgemental (whatever judgements are made are the pupils' own), self-referenced continuous process of recording. Within the RPA the recording was done on loose-leaf, titled cards (for example, Attendance, Group Project, Work, Hobby, Work Experience, Reading) which fitted into a record file. The records would be compiled within school time, normally in tutorial groups. An evaluation of the scheme (Swales, 1979) argued that personal recording had value for a variety of reasons. It had the potential to be a useful stimulus for curriculum development, to provide a sense of purpose for slow learners and to strengthen relationships between tutors and pupils. Drawbacks of the RPA were identified in the evaluation, one of which was that it was not regarded highly as a leaving qualification.[2] Nevertheless, personal records continued to evolve, with the Record of Personal Experience (RPE) branching off from the RPA in 1974. Further developments have included the Diamond Challenge introduced in 1977 (a variation of personal recording which involved pupils in developing personal programmes of work) and Pupils' Personal Records (PPR) which began in Wiltshire LEA in 1981. The principle of personal recording embodied in the original RPA scheme has been an extremely strong and widely spread influence on profiling systems. This is despite the strongly held view of one of the originators of personal recording, Don Stansbury, that personal recording and profiling are two very different and non-compatible entities. He perceives profiling as an extension of assessment and has argued that unfettered personal recording is not possible within a system of assessment (Stansbury, 1985).

---

[2] The term 'qualification' is retained here, rather than the less specific 'certificate', or even 'document', since all RPA literature uses the term.

Profiles have also developed within individual schools, though one of the earliest school-developed profiles, the Sutton Centre Profile, was influenced by the RPA. When the Centre opened in 1973 staff were keen to include a pupil personal record as one element of the overall profile. The Centre's profile has undergone two major revisions, the most recent being in 1983. This produced a system which was implemented in 1985. The profile itself consists of several card sheets kept in a loose-leaf binder. There are three sections: the first is the personal record compiled by the pupil with room for the tutor's comment. Secondly, there is the subject assessment record which includes pupils' self-assessments and teachers' assessments (both in the form of statements) and parents' comments. Thirdly, there is a record of external examination certificates. It is described as a three-way dialogue between pupils, teachers and parents. So here, pupils are involved not only in personal recording and in discussing this with their tutors, but they also take part in assessing their progress and achievement within the subjects they study.

Returning to Scotland, and a larger scale of development, at roughly the same time as the Sutton Centre first introduced their profile, a feasibility study was being carried out of a profile system which had been developed jointly by the Scottish Council for Research in Education (SCRE) and a Working Party of the Headteachers' Association of Scotland. The SCRE profile, as it became known, was made commercially available in 1976. It was aimed at the 60% of school leavers 'disenfranchised by the existing examination system' (Broadfoot, 1984b). (It should be noted that Scotland had never developed the CSE system in the way that England had, though some Scottish schools entered their pupils for English CSE examinations.) With the SCRE system the teacher recorded pupil achievement on a four-point, criteria-related, numerical scale in the 'basic skills' of listening, speaking, reading, writing, visual understanding and expression, use of number, physical co-ordination and manual dexterity. In addition, teachers recorded in the same way assessments of subject skills they had chosen. A section for the work-related skills of 'enter-prise' and 'perseverance' was included and these were rated on the four-point scale. It was hoped that the profile would encourage a dialogue between teacher and pupil, provide a cumulative record of progress and feed into a school leaving report (designed as part of the SCRE system). The SCRE profile was, perhaps, the first well known criteria-related, skills checklist. Although one of the functions of the SCRE system was to assist with pupil guidance, the format and content of the profile seem to have been designed with outside user's needs – particularly those of employers – uppermost in the developers' minds. A graphic and symbolic format was chosen for quick comprehension and evaluation (SCRE, 1977, p. 22) and 'the selection of different skills was also governed by consideration of those qualities looked for in school leavers by employers' (op. cit., pp. 38–9). In practice the system proved time-consuming to operate and many schools were not attracted to it because of this.

The first well known school-developed profile which adopted the skills checklist format was the Evesham High School Personal Achievement Record (PAR). This was introduced at the school in September 1979. It is reported to have grown out of concern for the demoralizing effect which an examination-based curriculum had on the lower half of the 'ability' range. Thus, originally, the pupils who did not take up the PAR were '... largely the most able for whom it was never intended' (Duffy 1980). The target group widened over the years and in 1983 the PAR was said to '... provide fifth year pupils of all abilities with a record of their skills and achievements' (Bowring, 1983). The developers of the Evesham PAR declared that the RPA, Stansbury's RPE and the SCRE profile system had been sources of influence. Indeed, the PAR embodies a mix of pupil initiated recording together with predefined skills checklisting. At the start of the fifth-year all pupils receive a PAR to be completed by the end of the Spring term. Completion is voluntary. The PAR is a pocket-sized booklet containing skills listed on separate pages under headings such as 'Language Skills', 'Maths Skills', 'Practical Skills' and 'Personal and Social Skills'. Pupils can also list the subjects they have studied, their exam results and personal achievements at the back of the record. Pupils initiate the recording process when they are confident they have mastered a skill by asking a teacher to authenticate this. In some cases a test will be given. It was hoped that pupils would take their PARs with them to job and further education interviews. Prior to the launch of the record, the head of the school actively solicited local employers' interest and funding. The production of the booklets was funded by employer donations in its first year (1979–80) but out of school funds in its second year of operation. In its third year, after the LEA declined to provide funds, employers were approached again. In the year 1984–5 no employer money was forthcoming for the scheme.

By the early 1980s profiling schemes were trying hard to shake off their 'less-able only' label; a label which had been self-consciously adopted in the 1970s and has since proved difficult to remove. The RPA had been developed originally for ROSLA pupils who were not entered for public examinations; the SCRE profile and the PAR (originally) were focused at non-exam pupils. Personal records and profiles were seen as tools for organizing the work of these pupils, providing a source of motivation and a leaving document. Pupils entered for public examinations were not typically the target for these early records and profiles. Examination syllabuses organized their work, examination success was their source of motivation and examination certificates were their leaving documents. However, as outlined in Section 3.2.1, it became increasingly apparent by the early 1980s that the currency of examination certificates had become devalued, hence, their potential to motivate many young people diminished. Profiles strived to acquire a wider applicability, first as potential motivators for 'able' but disaffected and unmotivated pupils and, secondly, as a source of personalized information – in addition to examination certificates – advertising what unique abilities and experience a young person has to 'sell' in the competitive and shrinking market place for the talents and services of the young. Likewise, the commercial interest of the examining boards in a time of falling rolls and hence likely falling exam entries must not be neglected as a factor in the promotion of profiling for all school pupils and college students.

Up to this point, profile developments in the school sector were patchy. In 1981 the Schools' Council survey of profile reporting in secondary schools identified only 25 schools which were using profile reports (Balogh, 1982). Subsequently, the Schools' Council funded a project involving 21 schools in four LEAs to study their development of records of achievement (Goacher, 1983). It was not until 1982, when the University of Oxford Delegacy of Local Examinations announced the development of the Oxford Certificate of Educational Achievement (OCEA) that profiling took on a more co-ordinated appearance for secondary schools. Three groups are cooperating in the certificate's development: the Delegacy, the participating LEAs of Oxfordshire, Leicestershire, Somerset and Coventry, and the University of Oxford Department of Educational Studies. OCEA was described as '...an assessment system which would be more relevant to young people's needs in the foreseeable future than is the existing examination system' (Oxford Delegacy, 1983, p. 1). It is designed to '...offer a wide ranging response to the whole spectrum of achievement and experience at school' and to '...provide a means of expressing more of the complete person than is possible by focusing on narrow and isolated abilities' (Oxford Delegacy, 1984, p. 2). The certificate will have three components:

1 The P-component: a description of the student's experiences, attainments, interests and skills;
2 The G-component: a record of achievements within the curriculum. At the time of writing this will include achievements in English, Mathematics, Modern Languages and Science;
3 The E-component: a record of examination results.

For the P-component, student personal recording is advocated together with frequent personal reviews between tutors and students. Within the G-component, the formative use of assessment is stressed and students are encouraged to become involved both in self-assessment and in the discussion of their assessment with their teachers. The piloting of OCEA started in over 40 schools in the four participating LEAs in September 1985 and it is intended that OCEA will be launched nationally from September 1987.

One of the issues underpinning the development of profiling, the transition from school to working life, has now become a protracted affair of course, and transition has become a certificated process in itself. The DES proposed the Certificate of Pre-vocational Education (CPVE) in 1982 (DES, 1982) and the 1-year, full-time courses leading to this started in schools in September 1985. The main aim of courses leading to the CPVE is to:

> ...assist the transition from school to adulthood by further equipping young people with the basic skills, experiences, attitudes, knowledge and personal and social competencies required for success in adult life including work. (Joint Board for Pre-vocational Education, 1984, p. 9)

Assessment within the CPVE framework is being reported in profiles for formative and summative use. A broad-based curriculum of knowledge, skills, experiences and personal development needs to be matched by a broad-ranging assessment and recording system. Given the claims being made for it both by developers and enthusiastic users, profiling appears to fit the bill, though early experience with CPVE suggests the profiling procedures are difficult to operate, with the benefits in teacher–student relationships being reduced through the mechanistic reporting procedures to a list of 'can do' achievements which do not properly reflect the nature of the course of study or the quality of teacher–student encounters.

(b) Further education

In parallel with developments in schools, teachers and examiners in further education were also beginning to take an interest in profiling in the 1970s. In 1976 the Royal Society of Arts became the first national examining body to make profile certification available. It did so for its Vocational Preparation (General) Course. The profile system consisted of a continuous assessment record in the form of a clerical skills checklist together with student diaries and logbooks. The final profile certificate listed statements of competence which referred to the course objectives which the student had attained.

One of the most influential documents in bringing debates about profiling to national attention was published in 1979. The Further Education Curriculum Review and Development Unit (FEU) produced *A Basis for Choice* (FEU, 1979) which recommended a unifying curriculum framework for post-16, pre-employment courses in further education. Features of the proposed approach to assessment for these courses were that it should serve and not dominate the curriculum, be internal, to aid local curricula variety, be formative, and allow for student contributions. Profile reporting of the assessment information was suggested. In 1979 the FEU, in conjunction with the City and Guilds of London Institute (CGLI), developed a profile to fit the framework for pre-employment courses described in *A Basis for Choice* and it is in such work that one can see the relationship between youth unemployment, vocationalism and certification at its most apparent.

The profile had a grid format listing core skills and achievement in these skills in terms of hierarchically-ordered descriptors. In addition, there was space for tutors' comments on these achievements and on the student's work experience. This format served as the model for almost all of the profiles subsequently developed for post-16 vocational preparation courses and training. The CGLI with the Manpower Services Commission (MSC) adapted the format slightly and augmented it with a diary, a logbook and review sessions for use in the Youth Opportunities Programme in 1981 and, more recently, for use in the Youth Training Scheme. A further adaptation of it was used by the CGLI for its 365 Vocational Preparation (General) Courses launched in colleges and in some schools in 1982. The latest version of the CGLI grid-style profile is used in both their Foundation Courses and within the Technical and Vocational Education Initiative (TVEI) in schools. The further education sector has nurtured and popularized the FEU/CGLI grid style profile.

However, the format has had its critics. It has been argued that this type of profiling presents value judgements as objective facts, implicitly forces teachers to grade and categorize students rather than reflect real differences in achievement, and that courses may be restricted to covering only the easily assessable objectives appearing in the profile (cf. *Times Educational Supplement*, 1982, p. 12). Grid-style profiles have been further criticized for being predetermined and imposed upon the student rather than being negotiated with the student, for failing to recognize individual students' needs and individual progress, and for being difficult for users to interpret (Scottish Vocational Preparation Unit, 1982). At the heart of such criticisms is the issue of whether assessment and its reporting can be 'context-free'. The underlying logic of profile reporting is that students are likely to have strengths and weaknesses, and that these may vary over time, and across different contexts of application. Yet grid-style reporting can be said to predetermine what counts as the 'whole student' and implies that variation must be due to variation in character-traits, rather than variation in the intrinsic complexity of tasks and the conditions under which they are carried out.

Profiling initiatives in the further education sector have come from the examining boards. They have been largely concerned with reporting achievement in basic skills together with vocationally relevant skills and experience. The grid-style format has predominated. The history of profile development in the school sector illustrates that most early models were devised by individual schools in response to their specific needs and for their own use. The launch of OCEA was the first example of a more organized form of development activity on profiling for school use, but it was the launch of the DES funded pilot schemes in records of achievement in 1985 (through which both OCEA and CGLI received money for pursuing their work in schools) which was the most significant fillip for more co-ordinated development work in schools on a national scale.

3.3 DES policy statement on records of achievement

In July 1984 the DES issued *Records of Achievement: A Statement of Policy*. In it Sir Keith Joseph (Secretary of State for Education, 1981–6) and his colleague (Secretary of State for Wales) expressed concern about the fact that most young people complete secondary education'... with no comprehensive record of their educational attainments' (DES, 1984, p. 1). Although most 16 year olds leave school with some examination certificates, the policy statement pointed out that few possess a record which includes other achievements made during their school careers as well as experiences which reflect personal and social qualities. The intention of the policy statement was for schools, through records of achievement, to widen the range of recognized achievement beyond results in public examinations, help pupils improve their motivation and self-awareness, promote a curriculum which enables pupils to develop practical and social skills and to provide a leaving document which would be valued by employers and educational and training institutions. The statement then argued that '... more practical experience and piloting is needed, together with some central co-ordination' (para. 9, p. 2) and proposed funding pilot schemes nationally '... to cast light on how best to set about recording pupils' achievements and thus to prepare the way for the establishment of agreed principles and a framework of national policy which can provide the basis for introducing records of achievement throughout England and Wales' (para. 9, pp. 2–3). The intention is that records of achievement will be introduced nationally by 1990.

Nine 3-year pilot schemes were launched in 1985 involving the Inner London Education Authority, Suffolk, Essex, Dorset, Lancashire, Wigan, the East Midlands Group (Northamptonshire, Nottinghamshire, Lincolnshire, Derbyshire), the Welsh Joint Examinations Council and OCEA (Somerset, Oxfordshire, Coventry, Leicestershire). In addition to those schools taking part in the DES funded pilot schemes, individual schools have responded to developments by running their own independent and unfunded schemes as have LEAs, both individually and collaboratively (e.g. The Northern Partnership for Records of Achievement, NPRA).

Practical guidelines laid down in the policy statement are that:

1 Records of achievement should be for all pupils.
2 There should be regular dialogue between teachers and pupils to identify achievement, motivate pupils and to stimulate curriculum review.
3 Recording of achievement should be regular and systematic and involve the pupil.
4 The leaving document should include evidence of academic attainment in public examinations as well as evidence of pupils' non-examined achievements and experiences. It should provide information which is useful to employers, further education and higher education institutions.
5 The leaving document should be the property of the pupil and information in the document should not be used without the pupil's permission.

The policy statement thus contains a number of proposals which could initiate radical change in assessment and in pedagogy. The principles of assessment and certification being promoted are that they should be inclusive in terms of encompassing both a broad range of achievements and experiences and by being applicable to all pupils. Assessment and recording should be used formatively and should involve the pupil.

The feedback from assessment should encourage teachers in reviewing both the curriculum and their teaching methods. Furthermore, there is the recommendation that pupils should have the right of veto over the use of the information in their final record of achievement. However, while much is implied by such suggestions, the document stops short of advocating significant reorienting of schooling because nothing is said which challenges traditional values which emphasize academic achievement. The following section from the statement of policy reveals quite clearly that, first, the 'talented' and the 'gifted' are still perceived to be those with a fistful of examination certificates and, secondly, that the status of records of achievement derives from their inclusion of the academic:

> There should be no question of confining records of achievement to pupils expected to leave school with few, if any, examination certificates. Both the internal processes of reporting, recording and discussion and the kinds of achievement and qualities described in the summary record are equally relevant for pupils with greater and lesser talents and gifts. (DES, 1984, para. 14, p. 4)

What is even more intriguing is that despite the stated intention for records of achievement to include all kinds of achievements, skills, abilities and qualities, it is felt that '. . . the records of some young people will look rather thin' (para. 13, p. 4). Does this, perhaps, reveal that the DES lacks faith in its own proposals, with 'low achievers' bound to remain 'low achievers', whatever the rules of the game, or does it show that its statement of policy on records of achievement was never intended to be a plan for fundamental change? One explanation for some of the tensions, not to say contradictions, in the statement of policy is that records of achievement are being used as a stone with which to kill too many birds at once. It is suggested that they can increase pupil motivation and raise the sum total of achievement, demonstrate to taxpayers and ratepayers that their money is showing tangible returns and provide the kind of information that employers and other users are said to need to make selection decisions. In other words, their purpose is three-fold: to satisfy educational, political and economic demands. The question for which it is difficult to find the answer in the policy statement is which purpose has priority? In practice, such issues may well be settled by established practice combined with lack of resources. As Goldstein and Nuttall (1986) point out, the present range of assessment practice – including records of achievement – potentially gives rise to and can be accommodated by a hierarchy of achievement: the traditional hierarchy in which academic accomplishment is recorded a higher status than the practical and the affective.

The research into the school-based development of pupil profiling which will now be reported has explored the ways in which individual secondary schools are responding to this assessment 'initiative'. The findings from a number of case studies of secondary schools' profile developments, some working within a funded pilot scheme, others working outside such a context, suggest that while, on the one hand, the development and use of profiling has the potential to bring about constructive change not only in assessment but in the curriculum and in pedagogy too, on the other hand, the educational apparatus within which these activities are taking place exercises severe constraints on both the scope and the magnitude of change.

3.4 The school-based development and use of profiling

Schools embarking on their own development of profiling are likely to face two challenges simultaneously. First, profiling itself – that is accessing a wider range of achievements and reporting them succinctly – is new to the majority of teachers; secondly, while whole-school institutional development involving all staff from all subject departments is an idea which is currently very fashionable, the practice of it is still unfamiliar to most teachers. These challenges motivate some teachers but, equally, they can be viewed as the source of yet more demands on finite supplies of time and energy. By 1984, however, the profiling movement was spreading attractive messages about the positive pay-offs from formative and criteria-related assessment, teacher/pupil dialogue and detailed, comprehensive recording and reporting. Likewise, the DES was holding out the carrot of Educational Support Grant funding to hard-pressed local authorities. The potential gains to be made from introducing a profiling system seemed sufficiently great to encourage involvement in development work.

3.4.1 *Features of the context*

Some of the schools studied are working independently on their own, unfunded developments. Others are participating in one of the DES funded pilot schemes on records of achievement. The DES pilot scheme is promoting a 'school-focused' approach to the development of profiling. It is considered important within the scheme for individual schools to conduct their own development work (within a set of guiding principles), first, to enable the specific aims and needs of the school to be taken into account and, secondly, to enable the particular expertise of the staff to be utilized. The scheme's funding is being used largely to provide in-service training and support for teachers in the participating schools and virtually all secondary schools in the authority, along with some middle and special schools, are involved in the development. It is anticipated that staff involvement in the programme of work will generate interest and commitment and provide an experiential basis for professional development.

However, the school-based development of profiling places heavy demands on teachers. Curriculum review, the development of a range of assessment procedures and practices, the provision of training for colleagues, and the design and management of the development process are responsibilities which have been taken on by teachers in addition to their normal duties. Demands are also made upon resources to provide staff with non-contact time for development work. Additionally, any innovatory development is likely to provoke resistance among some teachers. Although there is much support for the development of profiling, there is some scepticism about its claims and, also, its practical utility. Thus many teachers have been reluctant, certainly initially, to get involved.

Much of the development work in the schools studied has been initiated and sustained either by individual teachers who have taken on or have been assigned a co-ordinator's role, or by groups of self-selected enthusiasts. These teachers have been the source of many of the ideas both for the content of the profiles themselves and for the design of the development process. These individuals received very little specific preparation for their key roles in the developments. Most of them, being senior teachers, drew on their past experiences of curriculum development to guide their work on profiling. But although in-service education and training (INSET) on profiling and the issues associated with its development and use has been provided, particularly in the funded scheme, these teachers have still found themselves in the vulnerable position of having to learn for themselves about profiles and profiling through trial and error at school level, while, at the same time, guiding and co-ordinating the work of others. In many respects this is an inherent tension of a school-based approach. Effective development obviously depends on teachers adapting general ideas to their own particular institutional setting. But equally, teachers will look to developments elsewhere for guidance and even, perhaps, direct instruction, when they are under so much pressure to 'deliver' curricular reform on so many fronts at once. The problem with profiling is that there are relatively few general models available, and those that are have often been developed in inappropriate settings or for restricted target groups. Equally, because profiling carries so many implications with regard to the curriculum and school organization, these have necessarily to be confronted at the level of the individual school. Thus, the school-based development of profiling implies that the teachers involved must in many respects 'invent' profiling, rather than simply be in the position of operationalizing an already extant entity.

A general characteristic of the work is that a considerable

amount of it has been done in teachers' own time. Many of the teachers in key roles in the developments would accept that some background reading and research out of school hours is not unreasonable. However, when time is made available during the working day for teachers to carry out research and development with colleagues, the gains are numerous. For example, by making time for research and development, the management of a school can indicate the importance and the value of the project, groups can often solve problems more quickly than individuals can working alone, and the enthusiasm and resourcefulness of individuals is more easily tapped if they are given time to work with others. Another important reason for incorporating development sessions into school time is to ensure that the knowledge and expertise of certain staff is passed on to others. Development work can come to a standstill if key people leave a school before full use has been made of them as sources of information and ideas.

A final feature of the context of recent developments is that of teacher action. The academic year of 1985–6 will be remembered for the long and drawn out teachers' dispute. Union sanctions precluding their members involving themselves in any duties other than lesson preparation, teaching and marking seriously affected the development of profiling. For a substantial part of the year development work was forced underground and only surfaced in isolated classrooms behind closed doors. Apart from disrupting the development activity, the dispute dented the morale of many teachers. Funded and unfunded schools faced similar disruptions to their work. In the schools participating in the DES funded pilot scheme, any additional work on Educational Support Grant projects was specifically targeted by the unions. The dispute meant that teachers made less use of the resources available to them (i.e. supply cover, INSET, and money for materials development) than they may have wished. When sanctions were relaxed towards the end of that academic year, development work resumed but initially with reduced vigour, particularly since GCSE had become a predominant concern by this time.

3.4.2 Discovering the complexities of profiling: start-up problems in one school

Before moving on to a broad, overall review of research findings, it is instructive to report on some initial reactions to the idea and practice of profiling in one school. The school in question is a large co-educational comprehensive. To begin with those involved perceived profiling in terms of a teacher-controlled product which was likely to involve yet more form-filling for them:

> ... my understanding is that profiling and records of achieve-

ment are all to do away with the situation where people were
leaving school and had nothing to show for themselves...
[and] ... will be particularly important to those children who
are not really academic at all...

... [we had] doubts really as to the outcome of the project...
great concern that we were going to be involved in a
tremendous amount of paperwork...

The reasons for engagement in such an initially unpromising
exercise were essentially expedient – if profiles were coming, then
teachers might as well glean some idea of what was involved –
though there was also some weary scepticism about yet another
educational bandwagon:

... profiling ... was ... announced with the leaded glove of
Keith Joseph – "by 1990 you are all going to have to do this
chums, so you'd better get started now"...

... I just sort of volunteered – I said "if it's got to be done I'd
like to be at the forefront"...

... I think also one has to say that we were very, very keen
not to jump on the bandwagon ... everybody must jump on,
it's a new idea, a new initiative, which eventually fizzles out
through lack of infrastructure ... lack of support...

Gradually, discussions about the curriculum and teaching
methods began to arise out of initial discussions about assessment,
with the emphasis of in-service provision being on what it was
that those involved *wanted* to assess (and by implication, teach)
rather than just how to assess it. Interestingly enough, though,
given the earlier discussion of the developing practice and public
face of profiling, as development work progressed the word 'profiling', while being instantly recognizable, was also identified as
carrying very negative connotations:

... the thing that put [us] off initially was the word "profiling"
and the word "assessment"... [John] turned round and said
"well this is ridiculous, if they'd told us it was about the
curriculum to start with, we'd have been much more keen to
get on with it"...

Likewise some of the more trendy, 'bandwagon' ideas which the
teachers felt were behind recording achievement had also pene-
trated the school before developments got underway, and constituted another layer of mediating scepticism which had to be
worked through:

... I was not particularly happy with a totally positive
approach. I wanted a full and rounded picture to pass to

employers – and that's how I saw it to start with, for employers . . .

. . . if you lobotomise the English language, so that you can only express. yourself positively . . . what does that say to people when they're asked to deal with problem children? . . . how can I say it, the kinds of compliments which aren't compliments at all . . .

Nevertheless, the link with curriculum and teaching methods did become established. A major feature of the second year of development work, however, was a growing awareness of the advent of GCSE and the involvement of some members of staff in GCSE in-service training. As such the links between profiling and GCSE coursework assessment at departmental level came to be perceived as particularly important and relevant, though perhaps at the expense of a wider whole-school review of curricular provision:

. . . when we were asked to look at profiling . . . I looked at the future proposed GCSE or 16+ exams, the syllabus, to see what the changes were, and I tried to break that down into small segments so that we could try and sort of make up a worksheet idea . . .

. . . the structured checklist we provided . . . was an attempt to clarify the skills which you can see are broken down into listening, reading, writing and speaking . . . we based our grading A, B, C, D, E, more or less on the demands of the GCSE assessment . . .

. . . the coursework's by learning assignments during the term . . . there are six assessed assignments which contribute 50% of the final mark . . . so we thought we could just profile the assessed assignments . . .

As GCSE drew closer then, profiling became locked into it, and particularly with the coursework elements. The major reason for this appears to be that of pragmatism. The staff were having to come to terms with what were in some cases major changes of syllabus and teaching method in GCSE. Any framework which rendered this more manageable was likely to be utilized.

GCSE has not prevented other work taking place, however, albeit on a small scale, and furthermore there are at least some of those involved who can envisage profiling having a much more profound effect on the school. But developing an understanding of the potential, and hence the complexities, of profiling, does not necessarily lead to ready solutions to the sorts of issues which it raises. Discovering complexity in action has certainly revealed the issues to which commentators have drawn attention, and about which the DES seeks data; indeed, the process of generating an understanding of the issues is clearly a good deal more subtle and time-consuming than many policy makers, may have imagined, but the process also generates an appreciation of the enormity of the task and some doubt over how best to proceed:

> ...there are things which are going to be very difficult to assess...things like "can make decisions in a rational manner leading to successful outcomes"...I think that's the crux of profiling, rather than just ticking off "has been able to press certain keys". But how did somebody make a rational decision?...How do you assess that?...These are...not the things that we've had the time or that we've got the expertise to thrash out...

> ...we've developed...our...marking scheme...the problem we have currently is that we want to be able to discuss our marking with the pupils...if you have one double lesson per group there really isn't any way of doing it...you've got to discuss the work they've done and... try to get some feedback from them as to what they think of the quality of their work and still actually have a useful lesson going on at the same time...

The very nature of what it is schools are trying to achieve, and by what means they should try to achieve it, are put under scrutiny by such comments, but the practical implications for how best to make progress are by no means clear. Similarly, there is no sense in which teachers in this school are simply 'trying out' profiling, in order to better understand how to 'do it'. The nature of the beast changes with growing experience. Thus profiling means different things to different teachers, and their ambitions and perceptions of what would count as successful practice vary accordingly.

Having said this, however, it is also the case that the school is beginning to try to make more general headway. General issues such as the provision of more tutor time and the replacement of current reporting procedures by arrangements which would accommodate profiling more readily are being discussed. Thus, it is clear that this school's involvement with profiling in what was originally something of a 'watching brief', has generated a dynamic of its own, and something of an understanding of profiling and a commitment towards it has developed. However, substantial and coherent whole-school developments still remain elusive.

As regards those most involved, some are eager to pilot work in their own departments and continue learning from experience:

...at the moment I think we need to run our own profile, then evaluate it...really to see how successful the whole exercise is...

...what we might do...is to say "right, we'll start and make a mess of it" – right, we've learnt from the mess rather than not done anything...rather than just to keep waiting. I think you can keep waiting to start and you might never start...

Wilmott (1986), reporting on development work in OCEA, has suggested that 'it may be that if the job is worth doing it is worth doing badly in the first instance (Wilmott, 1986, p. 133). He means presumably that any experience of putting profiles into practice must be worthwhile: we all learn from our mistakes. But while this may be true enough in some senses, it also needs to be remembered that mistakes can have consequences. Certainly there are other teachers at this particular school for whom caution is as important as commitment, and indeed may even be said to stem from it:

...we want this instrument of policy for the department but we want to do it properly, we don't want it just on paper because it looks good, we want to really work it through ...don't automatically assume that we've got to start putting little ticks in boxes until we know why we've got the boxes in the first place and whether it's actually relevant...

...I still find it difficult to know how you are going to give a full assessment with sensible profiling with groups over fifteen...you can't just say "right get on with that" [written work] because it's a pointless task and we are constantly being urged not to set pointless tasks...

...I thought at first..."why don't County get one sorted our for us and then send it down and we'll just put it into practice", the moment you get over that first hurdle of profiling and you start to understand it, you realise that that's probably the worst thing that could possibly be done... [profiling]...is probably the next priority, but only in so much as it's going to help the kids. We're not going to do it for profiling's sake, which is what I've sometimes forgotten. I've thought "gosh, we've got a meeting coming up, I'd better get some sort of profile", without any regard for does it help the pupils with their work?...

For the moment then, we can speculate that profiling will continue to take root and develop in this school, but in directions which are still open to change and at a pace which may frustrate some policy-makers. Developing an understanding of profiling takes time, and in itself throws up as many questions as answers, which in turn need to be addressed with care. In this case a growing understanding of the innovative potential of profiling, juxtaposed with the manifest exigencies of examination-oriented school organization, is generating considerable caution.

3.4.3 *General lessons from the development work*

Moving on from the particular to the general, it is clear that profiling was initially perceived by many teachers primarily as an improved method of reporting, and indeed some teachers had discussed and experimented with changes in reporting prior to the start of their schools' profiling projects. Much early development work involved teachers in drafting and testing more detailed subject reports in profile format, i.e. containing information on subject content covered as well as the subject specific and cross-curricular skills promoted in the courses.

It is not surprising that teachers should tackle the development of profiling from the reporting angle. First, the summative, end-product of the assessment and profiling process is the only tangible part which is readily communicable to novitiates. A teacher looking to existing schemes for profiling ideas, will inevitably come across products rather than processes. What is most easily known and understood about, for example, the Evesham PAR, is its content and format. What is more difficult to ascertain are the processes of assessment and discussion which precede recording. Secondly, the emphasis in the DES policy statement on *records* of achievement (as against, for example, record*ing* achievement) is implicitly, and at times explicitly placed on the summative stage of the profiling process. Of course this element is important, but the evidence reported here suggests that until the processes of formative assessment and recording are firmly established, there is little chance of a school producing a valid and reliable summative profile. If teachers make no changes in their pedagogical and assessment practices, there can be no change in the nature and scope of the information they are able to provide.

Interestingly enough, however, teachers' early preoccupations with reporting assessment gradually gave way to concerns about assessment itself. It was when teachers were asked by colleagues to fill in profiles listing skills and abilities they had never assessed that questions about how to assess them, and what implications this carried for classroom organization and teaching methods, arose. Although teachers were not having to invent new methods of assessment, they were having to try methods of which they had little, or no, previous experience, and in a rapidly changing assessment environment.

Teachers have always assessed pupils, though often, particularly with regard to attitude and motivation, in a very informal and often judgemental fashion, and with little in the way of hard evidence. Most internal tests and external examinations are concerned with the recall of knowledge presented in written answers to written questions. Now teachers are being asked to assess not only knowledge but also the pupil's understanding of what they learn and their ability to apply their knowledge. Skills and abilities which have not in the past been assessed in written examinations are now targets for assessment not only within pupil profiling schemes but also within initiatives such as GCSE, TVEI and CPVE. GCSE requires teachers to assess not only what pupils know but also what they 'understand and can do'. The scope of assessment is widened to include not only the recall of factual information but also the pupil's ability to apply knowledge learnt. Teachers are having to assess pupils on a range of skills and abilities which cannot readily be tested by written examinations, e.g. research skills, the ability to work in groups, the ability to make and record accurate observations, motor skills, oral skills, investigational, planning and design skills. For pupils completing TVEI courses, teachers will have to provide a record of achievement showing attainments which are not included within the range of qualifications pupils gain. Teachers are having to assess and record what pupils learn during work experience and residential education. Teachers are also being required to assess and discuss with pupils their 'personal development'. Within CPVE courses teachers are required to assess pupils' use of 'process skills' which are promoted through the CPVE core, e.g. analysis and problem solving, social skills and practical skills. Pupils' competence in 'vocational skills' are to be assessed to national, industrial standards. Furthermore, teachers are expected to assess whether or not pupils have developed 'appropriate attitudes' for their adult and working lives.

Teachers have to find new sources of evidence for this expanding range of achievements, abilities and skills. An element in many of the subject profiles tested in the schools studied is skills assessment. Many subject departments reviewed the aims and content of their courses during their work on profiling. As a result, they identified more clearly the knowledge, subject-specific skills and cross-curricular skills which they wanted the courses to promote and which pupils were being expected to learn. Many of the skills and attributes being assessed are those which can only be demonstrated by a pupil during the process of working or while carrying out a practical task, e.g. verbal communication, observation, manual dexterity in handling equipment, leadership and cooperation. Teachers are, therefore, experimenting with the observation and recording of these skills in the classroom as work is in progress, while also reorienting their teaching to try to ensure that pupils have the opportunity to demonstrate 'cooperation' or whatever.

Various skills checklists have been devised to aid observation. Even though many teachers argue that observation of, for example, group work and practical work is the only method of assessment which will provide information on certain skills and abilities, few teachers report that they employ observational methods of assessment effectively. For a start, inadequate training in assessment contributes to many teachers' initial lack of confidence. But there are many practical constraints too. Teachers have found that using observation methods with large groups means that assessment is prolonged over weeks before all pupils are assessed on all of the skills. Issues of the effectiveness of formative feedback are obviously raised by such problems. Furthermore, in science subjects, teachers can have difficulties when trying to observe and assess one or two pupils and not being able to monitor the remaining 20 who may be involved in potentially dangerous activities. Effective use of the observation of practical and group work relies on pupils within the class possessing sufficient self-discipline to work unsupervised for certain periods while the teacher concentrates on observing and assessing a small group. In many respects, then, teachers are relying on the attributes which they are trying to develop and assess – self-reliance for example – already being present in their teaching groups. Even if almost perfect conditions prevail – that is, a small group, safe activities and good pupil self-discipline – a teacher has to display considerable ingenuity to juggle the roles of work facilitator, group monitor and assessor all at the same time. Observational assessment can be made easier and more effective if two or more teachers work as a team with one group of pupils. This demands flexible timetabling and, were it to be instituted on anything more than an 'experimental' basis, more generous staffing than is available in most schools.

A feature of many profiling schemes is the inclusion of pupil self-assessment. The DES policy statement on records of achievement recommends that the processes of assessing and recording should involve the pupil. Teachers in the schools studied have been working on ways in which pupils can contribute to their own assessment. However, pupil self-assessment has not been greeted by all teachers as a positive development. Some teachers have questioned both its value and its purpose, believing that their assessments and those of external examiners are what ought to count. There is also disagreement over the ability of pupils to assess their own achievements. Some teachers have argued that, for example, 11 and 12 year olds are not mature enough to carry out self-assessment. Such attitudes clearly derive from and reinforce longstanding practices and will impact on the effectiveness of 'self-assessment' even if it does become part of any national guidelines. The view that inarticulate pupils and those with literacy problems will not be able to contribute confidently to recording and discussing self-assessments has also been expressed.

However, despite the reservations, pupil self-assessment has been tested in a range of departments in the schools studied. In science, for example, pupils in one school carry out their own assessment of practical work and record this on a skills record sheet. These are handed in and the teacher records his/her assessment of the pupil's work together with comments on the pupil's self-assessment. These sheets are returned to the pupils and are discussed if necessary in lesson time. One mathematics department has been encouraged to try pupil self-assessment partly as a result of the new assessment demands in GCSE mathematics. The staff have used a questionnaire to elicit pupils' comments and views on their performance in mathematics, on the course content and on the teaching approach used. The initial fear of some of the teachers involved, that pupils would make personal attacks on staff in their comments, was not realized. In fact, most found pupils' comments constructive and illuminating. In another school, pupils carry out periodic reviews of their work in their humanities course and then record their own assessment of their progress over half a term. Because the reviews cover a number of weeks of work, pupils can reflect more broadly not only on individual pieces of work or activities but also on patterns emerging in their learning and achievement, on the course itself and on what targets they should be aiming for in the following weeks. Their assessments, comments and targets are commented upon by their teacher who can also contribute suggestions for remedial work or for future activities.

Most teachers who have experimented with pupil self-assessment have found the information resulting from it to be relevant and useful. Pupil comments can reveal problems, and the sources of problems, which are invisible to the teacher. They can also provide valuable feedback about the appropriateness and popularity of certain teaching methods, topics and the pace of teaching. Also, by giving over some of the responsibility for assessment to pupils, teachers can relieve some of the burden on themselves. Positive effects experienced by pupils can be greater involvement in lessons and increased confidence when their assessment is taken notice of and when they are encouraged to be less negatively critical of themselves. But pupil self-assessment on its own is by no means a magic cure for unmotivated pupils. Indeed, for any positive effects to accrue from the activity it must be planned properly in advance, and in this respect teachers in the schools studied are very much learning on their feet. Their work has highlighted that: (1) the purposes of self-assessment must be made clear to the pupils. These purposes may be to help the pupil identify strengths and weaknesses, to help the pupil decide what kind of help he/she needs, to involve the pupil more in the learning process, to give the pupils some responsibility for planning their work and for deciding targets, and to provide teachers with feedback. (2) The language and criteria used in pupil self-assessments sheets must be understandable to them. (3) Pupils must feel that self-assessment is more than just a dialogue with themselves. The information must be commented upon by teachers, discussed and used to improve what the school is offering to its pupils. This is perhaps the most challenging feature of profiling – when and how to act upon information gathered.

A key word in many approaches to profiling is 'negotiation'. In, for example, the GCLI 365 Vocational Preparation (General) Course negotiation is done in three ways. The students negotiate with staff, first, which vocational areas they should study to suit their needs, secondly, how they will tackle the planned work programmes and, thirdly, the assessment of their progress. The stated intention is for students to raise questions about their programmes of work and to negotiate with staff relevant changes. In the DES policy statement on records of achievement it is suggested that there should be 'regular dialogue' between teachers and pupils. Dialogue does not necessarily imply negotiation of course and, in fact, the scope for negotiation in secondary schools is considerably more limited than it is in the post-compulsory sector. Negotiation between teachers and pupils in the schools studied is largely confined to one or two courses where pupils, as a group, can make a joint decision with the teachers concerned about the topics to be covered. But the organization and structure of most secondary schools cannot support the kind of individualized learning within which negotiation would have real meaning. Some discussion between teachers and pupils about progress, problems, achievements and targets is taking place, but it is limited in scope, and even then has run into problems. Some subject teachers have tried, for example, to discuss with individual pupils the comments they have made on the pupils' homework. Despite the simplicity of the exercise, two main factors impinge upon its smooth running. First, large groups of over 30 pupils mean that such discussion, as far as individuals are concerned, is infrequent. Secondly, as the discussion has to take place in the classroom, there is little privacy and confidentiality.

A defining characteristic of profiles is the inclusion of assessments or evidence of a pupil's personal and social skills or qualities. This type of assessment or comment appears under various headings on summative profiles, e.g. as 'attitudes', 'personal and social skills', 'personal qualities', or 'social abilities'. Reference is made, for example, to pupils' self-awareness, ability to work with others, self-reliance, cooperativeness, perseverance, punctuality, confidence, honesty and reliability. Arguments for such a section in a profile have included the fact that in many schools' written aims these capacities are said to be promoted and, therefore, should be reported; that this type of assessment or comment is valued by selectors for further education and employment; that these skills or qualities influence the way in which pupils learn and achieve and therefore should be referred to. There is also some residual feeling that profiles are for the apparently less academic and as such it is precisely pupils' personal qualities on which they should be concentrating: she may be a 'poor examinee' but she's a 'good kid'. Some teachers have, however, expressed reservations about attempting to assess and record these because, for example, they are not trained to make what they see as personality judgements; their judgements will be personal and subjective and, therefore, of limited value; there is likely to be disagreement among teachers about the meaning of personal skills categories and descriptors; and that they have no right to pressure pupils into making personal disclosures.

These problems return us to the issue of context and the extent to which teachers perceive assessment, particularly social and personal assessment, as located within a psychological – perhaps it would be more accurate to say psychometric – frame of reference, rather than a sociological or educational one. Within the traditional psychometric model that which is assessed is construed in terms of individual ability and reported without reference to test conditions – to the context of assessment. Thus 'honesty', to take a particularly acute example, is taken to be a character trait adhering to individuals rather than a product of particular situations, or, more convincingly, a combination of both. Small wonder that many teachers doubt their capacity to assess such traits, though even more worrying, some teachers have been encountered who do *not* doubt their own capabilities in this area. From a more sociological or educational perspective the issue of context – the context of learning and assessment – is crucial. Such a perspective would also recognize that the perceptions of educational encounters held by assessor and assessed can vary with respect to race, gender and social class. The practical implications of this perspective would involve teachers and pupils being able to report and reflect on what has happened, in certain circumstances, without necessarily implying that it will always happen in every circumstance. Even so, in all of the schools studied teachers have included the assessment and recording of personal and social capabilities in the profiles they have been following, and these have usually been construed as generalizable traits of individuals. In some cases this type of assessment or evidence gathering has been left to the form tutors or confined within the schools' personal and social education programmes, but there are examples of subject teachers accepting responsibility for assessing and recording these items. The process of gathering information about personal and social skills has varied. Sometimes the basis for assessment and recording is simply the teacher's overall 'gut feeling' about the pupil which is then translated into grades or comments for specific skills. The process can be more systematic and some teachers have included personal and social skills in their observation checklists which they use periodically to gather assessment information on their pupils. But this more systematic evidence gathering must still attend to issues of assessor–competence and/or bias. Some teachers have used the pupils' own personal self-assessments as the basis for any personal and social skills record, but this is by no means widespread practice in the schools studied.

The recording of such information has been done in a variety of ways. There are examples from the schools of personal and social skills checklists on which teachers record grades. In some cases brief explanations of the grades are written by the teacher, or grade descriptors are listed on the checklists. Another approach which has been used is the recording of comments by the teacher against skill headings. In most cases, personal and social assessments made by teachers are not based on recorded evidence, are categorized under predetermined headings and are recorded either in terms of grades or as cryptic descriptors. This raises a number of questions. For example, are teachers always the best source of information on a pupil's personal and social skills – what about out-of-school activities? Does the pupil have valuable evidence and comment to contribute which is not being tapped? If assessments or comments are not based upon recorded evidence, how can they be relied upon and explained if they are questioned? Does the use of predetermined personal and social skills categories on record sheets and checklists simply give a spurious validity to the labelling and stereotyping of pupils rather than encourage and facilitate the description of pupils' individuality? (cf. Stronach, 1986, for a much more detailed analysis of such possibilities).

With more assessment information being collected and used formatively, some teachers feel that it is now important to meet with colleagues both to discuss the progress of individual pupils and of groups and to agree relevant changes in courses and in pupil groupings. The statement of policy on records of achievement issued by the DES recommends that assessment information and feedback from teacher/pupil dialogues should stimulate curriculum review. In some of the schools, staff in certain subject departments have free time blocked together. This facilitates discussion and also enables teachers to pursue further their assessment and profiling development work. Where this does not operate, meetings between teachers occur too casually and too infrequently to provide a firm basis for curriculum review. It is extremely difficult for teachers to maximize the use of assessment information if the discussion of it is not built into the timetable.

A time-consuming and labour intensive element of profiling is the recording of assessment information. One of the main drawbacks of many profiling systems is that the compilation of the assessment records often takes an inordinate amount of time. For example, a major weakness of the SCRE profile system was that the detailed recording it required was too time-consuming to be workable. In further education and in the Youth Training Scheme, recording for the FEU/CGLI grid-style profiles can be so demanding of time that often the system cannot be maintained properly. Despite the evidence against lengthy and elaborate recording, there have been examples of it in all of the schools studied. In the early stages of profile development work teachers perceived the essential characteristics of profiles to be their detail and their bulk. Early drafts of profiles often ran into several pages, involved a number of contributors and spanned the academic and the affective domains and everything in between. After the trial was completed, such records were almost always trimmed back or in some cases abandoned. Teachers were then forced into asking questions about the scope, detail and format of assessment records, and the frequency of their compilation and their intended audiences. These are not easy questions to answer.

One of the major issues in need of some debate is the distinction between formative recording and summative reporting. Formative records are essentially internal working documents, continuously updated and amended, for use by both teacher and pupil to encourage, guide and reward learning and to stimulate reviews of the curriculum and pedagogy by informing teachers of the effectiveness of teaching methods and the appropriateness of what is taught. Summative reports are static, end-of-stage (-term,-course,-year,-school career) documents which present a distillation of all the assessment information available about a pupil geared, both in terms of content and format, to the needs or interests of audiences outside the school, e.g. parents, employers, colleges, training schemes. Although it would not be possible to generate numerous types of record and report to serve different audiences and purposes, teachers need to acknowledge the differences between formative recording and summative reporting in order to select, edit and communicate assessment information appropriately and effectively to the various users of that information. Training is needed to enable teachers to make full use of formative records during the processes of teaching and learning and to produce summative reports from the information and evidence gathered.

The assessment, recording, discussion and reporting which make up the profiling process all take time. While teachers are testing new approaches, but are still having to maintain traditional practices until the alternatives become replacements for these, the demands on their time can be considerable. But even when they are established on their own, formative assessment, pupil/teacher dialogue and broad ranging and detailed continuous recording will be time-consuming procedures. It is not simply a question of bolting on an extra 20 or 30 minutes at the end of the school day to allow for these to be done. The nature of the assessment and recording processes necessitates their integration within teaching and learning time. The issue is fundamentally one of the organization and use of time and is associated with how teachers teach and how the school day and week are arranged. As long as teaching and learning are organized on the basis of individual teachers working with groups of around 30 pupils in periods of 35 or 70 minutes, the space to reorient assessment and recording will be restricted.

Changes have been made in the timetables of some of the schools studied to allow for the new demands of profile development and operation. For example, as mentioned earlier, some departments have free time blocked to enable the subject team to meet to discuss assessment and to plan change. In one school, some form tutors have been given an extra 70-minute period every week during which they can withdraw tutees from other lessons for one-to-one discussions. Some English departments have timetabled all English lessons in a particular year at the same time so that a team of teachers works with the whole year group. This confers a certain amount of flexibility by enabling a variety of activities to take place simultaneously. For example, a large group can be viewing a film or a video while some pupils are involved in self-directed small-group work and some pupils have one-to-one discussions with teachers who are freed by their colleagues from facilitating and supervising groups. Extra staffing is an obvious, though rare, bonus which facilitates more flexible timetabling. One English department has been using a part-time teacher to work alongside other English teachers in lessons. This has enabled one teacher to concentrate on individual pupils or on small groups for the purposes of observation, assessment and discussion.

The complexity and the difficulty of developing profiling in today's secondary schools is all too apparent from the research evidence reviewed here. Despite the difficulties and the unresolved issues there remains, as highlighted in Section 3.4.2, considerable if qualified support for profiling. There is commitment among teachers in the schools studied to the establishment of comprehensive assessment, recording and reporting systems. The task is not simple. Certain conditions would seem to be essential for promoting the kind of changes the DES policy statement on records of achievement recommends schools to make in order to improve the assessment, recording and reporting of pupil achievement. These are outlined in the final section of this chapter. Taken together they carry significant resource implications. Some of these can be met by re-ordering priorities within the boundaries of the school, some by reorienting current in-service provision. Nevertheless, substantial additional funds have been utilized in the DES's pilot schemes and it should also be noted that one of the 'unfunded' schools referred to here has had access to additional resources through involvement in TVEI. For profiling to be implemented effectively, and the quality of teacher–pupil encounters sustained in the longer term, there can be little doubt that extra resources, particularly in the form of extra staff and hence smaller teaching groups, will be necessary.

3.5 Facilitating and sustaining change

1 *A review of school aims and curricular intentions* is useful for establishing a baseline from which development work can start. What range of skills, capacities and attitudes is the school currently trying to develop in pupils? Do new or additional learning opportunities have to be provided to meet these aspirations?

2 *A review of existing assessment, recording and reporting practices* can continue the process. Such reviews can identify which elements of practice are unsatisfactory and in need of change as well as revealing examples of good practice which could be retained, strengthened and disseminated more widely within the school.

3 *The establishment of a school assessment policy* can help to identify and clarify the scope of assessment, recording and reporting, the principles upon which they should be based and the purposes

they should serve. It is upon such a policy that a coherent framework for change can be based.

4   *INSET* will be necessary which provides: (i) practical, classroom-based help with assessment, recording and reporting methods and with the formative use of assessment information, and (ii) guidance and support for teachers in key co-ordinating and leadership roles to help them manage the development process.

5   *Non-contact time* is important for teachers during development work for the process of review, materials development and for subsequent reflection and planning with colleagues. During the operation of formative assessment and recording, teachers need non-contact time blocked with departmental colleagues to discuss, for example, possible curriculum changes. They also need such time for pupil counselling which is part of formative assessment.

6   *More flexible teaching methods*, facilitating individual and small group work, as well as whole-class teaching, will then be an integral and necessary part of any substantial change.

7   *Timetable changes* can then facilitate more effective formative assessment and teacher/pupil discussion. Year groups can be timetabled together for a particular subject with a teaching team so that certain teachers can be freed for more one-to-one and small-group observation and assessment. Blocking the timetable, at least in some subjects, in morning and afternoon sessions on a fortnightly cycle can provide teachers with more flexibility to integrate teaching, observation, assessment and discussion than, for example, 35- or 70-minute periods provide.

8   *The restructuring of the accommodation* of some schools would help in the provision of small private rooms for teacher/pupil discussions and to provide suitable space for staff both to work privately and to meet with colleagues for discussions, curriculum review and INSET.

Chapter 4

The Development, Use and Impact of Graded Tests*

David Pennycuick

4.1 Introduction

Graded test schemes have frequently arisen because of dissatisfaction with traditional methods of teaching and examining. Since the mid-1970s many schemes have been developed, particularly in modern languages, and proponents of these schemes appear to have five main criticisms of public examinations. Only the first of these is subject-specific.

1 Examination syllabuses have been based on language structure (i.e. grammar) rather than on the use of language to communicate, and therefore have been inappropriate for most pupils.
2 Traditional examinations have had too long a time-span (up to 5 years) before any results have been achieved. Shorterterm objectives would, it is claimed, lead to a higher degree of motivation.
3 The use of norms to determine grade boundaries has led to a sense of failure on the part of most candidates.
4 Public examination results have not reported clearly exactly what candidates can do.
5 Examinations have been designed only for the top 60% of the ability range, and there has been no provision for the rest.

Graded test schemes attempt to overcome these criticisms by means of three key features which may be called level-

*This chapter is adapted from parts of Pennycuick and Murphy (1988). Some of the content also appears in Pennycuick (1987).

progression, success-orientation and curriculum-linking. These features are incorporated in the following definition:

> In a graded test scheme, there is a sequence of tests at progressive levels of difficulty, complexity, sophistication and/or syllabus content, which are designed to be taken by students only when they have a high probability of success. Each test is closely linked to the curriculum for the relevant level by means of clear specification of the knowledge and processes to be assessed and of the standards to be attained. (Pennycuick, 1986)

While the graded test movement has been most prominent in modern languages, as a result of local initiatives by groups of secondary school teachers, there are operational schemes in several other subject areas — mathematics, science, music, physical education and business studies. Some are longstanding, for example the music examinations of the Associated Board of the Royal Schools of Music, which are often cited as a model for the development of schemes of Graded Objectives in Modern Languages (GOML). Other well-established schemes include the Kent Mathematics Project, and the shorthand and typewriting examinations of the Royal Society of Arts and the Pitman Institute. There are also several similar developments in progress under the broader heading of graded assessment (Harrison, 1985).

For the purposes of this chapter no distinction will be made between the terms graded tests, graded objectives and graded assessment. However, while most schemes share the three key features and thus satisfy the above definition, it must be pointed out that there is great variety among schemes, even within the same subject area, and that those responsible for their development would not necessarily have the same priorities. It is therefore important to beware of over-generalization. In addition, all three key features are to some extent problematic, and graded testing gives rise to a wide range of curricular, pedagogic, psychological, technical and administrative issues. For a fuller treatment than is possible here, see Pennycuick and Murphy (1988); the development of GOML schemes is also described by Harding *et al.* (1980) and by Harrison (1982).

4.2 Mastery, criterion-referencing and level-progression

Although some definitions of graded tests use terms such as mastery and criterion-referencing, they have been avoided in the definition presented above, since graded test schemes rarely satisfy the wide and precise range of conditions specified by models for criterion-referenced assessment (e.g. Popham, 1978) or for mastery learning programmes (e.g. Bloom, 1974). Nevertheless, graded tests have much in common with these models, at any rate in principle. Once the syllabus, tests and pass criteria are decided for each level of a particular graded test scheme, then pupil performance is assessed in relation to the set standard determined by those criteria, not in relation to the performance of other pupils. Graded tests are designed to emphasize assessment functions other than discrimination. However, syllabus objectives, test items and pass marks are decided with the intention that they should be appropriate for the target group of pupils so that the great majority might experience success. Norms implicit in the minds of members of groups developing graded test schemes can be a major factor in determining the content of each level.

Clear specification of standards is not always straightforward; it is easier to achieve for performances in (say) athletics, or for objective written tests, than in a field where judgement by an assessor is required, as in oral language tests or practical music examinations. But, however it is accomplished, specification of standards is dependent upon first defining the tasks to be performed; in many cases designers of graded test schemes achieve this through behavioural objectives.

Most graded tests lead to the award of marks, and most (although not all) specify pass marks. However, it is not always easy to decide on a cut-off score to separate 'masters' from 'non-masters'. Clearly this must be a high score if mastery is to be associated with success, and if we wish to know with a high degree of precision what successful candidates can do. But teachers and pupils are unlikely to favour very high cut-off points, for motivational reasons and also because the higher the pass mark the more precisely the tasks to be mastered must be specified, thus reducing course flexibility. Bloom (1976) states that 'mastery is frequently defined as something approximating 80 to 85% of the items on a criterion-referenced test', but the level defined as mastery in a graded test scheme would not be regarded as satisfactory unless a large proportion of candidates do in fact succeed. In a GOML scheme which uses 'intelligibility to a sympathetic native speaker' as a criterion of success, it might be felt that a pass mark of about 60% is appropriate, since pupils who can do that percentage of the specified tasks would 'get by' in relevant situations. Although there is a sense in which mastery levels are arbitrary, in practice they must not be either too high or too low. Some schemes avoid the dilemma caused by simultaneous requirements for high pass marks and high pass rates by having more than one cut-off score. For example, the School Science Certificate scheme awards both Silver and Gold certificates at each level. In other schemes mastery requirements include hurdles for separate test components.

In the background of graded test schemes are the following principles:

1   Assessment is designed to determine whether or not mastery has been attained.
2   Pupils should only be entered for tests when they are likely to succeed.
3   Candidates should master one level before proceeding to the next.

However, in practice, application of these principles is not always straightforward, and pragmatic considerations, such as the need to keep a class together, may predominate. Although graded test schemes may be perceived in terms of mastery learning, this is not necessarily prominent in the minds of teachers.

4.3 Success-orientation

The principle that pupils should only be entered for tests when they are likely to succeed may be referred to as the *principle of readiness*. Several possible strategies for implementing this principle are discussed by Pennycuick and Murphy (1988). One is individualized learning, which is applied, for example, in the Kent Mathematics Project. Another is vertical timetabling (see Penny-cuick, 1985), in which pupils are allocated to classes not by virtue of their age, but according to their level of attainment in the relevant subject. Both these strategies have much to recommend them if it is felt important for teaching and learning to be success-oriented. However, the majority of graded test schemes are based on class teaching in the context of traditional British schooling, in which class allocation is by age and classes may be mixed-ability, particularly in lower secondary forms.

The use of class teaching methods may mean that the class will not be ready to take tests at the same time, unless some device is used to ensure that the rates of progress of all class members are reasonably equal. For example, Bloom's 'Learning for Mastery' strategy allows slower students to keep up with the group by the use of 'instructional correctives' outside the regular class time. Another possible device is for the teacher to proceed at the pace of the slower students and provide extra 'extension' work for the faster members of the class. Or it might be possible for the course to cover all the objectives for several graded test levels and pupils to be entered for tests appropriate for each individual. Certainly logistic constraints on both teaching and testing mean that where graded test schemes are designed for a class teaching approach it is likely that the teacher will decide to arrange for the whole class to be tested at the same time. Such constraints may well require a compromise on the principle of readiness even if one of the above devices is adopted. Apart from differences in individual rates of progress, teachers must judge when they feel the class as a whole is ready, and school organizational factors (e.g. internal examinations or the end of a term) may intervene. But if success-orientation is to be achieved, flexibility in course timing is essential.

If pupils do take tests before they are ready, they will fail to reach the set standard. The principles of mastery learning then require the provision of appropriate remedial assistance followed by the opportunity to retake tests, before moving on to the next level. This may be difficult to organize in practice, and a teacher faced with a situation in which perhaps one-third of the class have failed, the remainder having passed, is in somewhat of a dilemma. This may be resolvable in some circumstances if a setting system is in operation, or the teacher may arrange extra lessons out of normal school time for the failures. But teachers who do not give particularly high priority to the mastery learning aspects of graded test schemes may decide to move on to work for the next level with the whole class regardless of the fact that some have failed, although that would of course dilute the intended emphasis on success.

Readiness is only one aspect of success-orientation. Another factor is the design of the tests themselves. Since it is not necessary for them to discriminate between candidates, it is possible for items to have very high facility indices. Thus graded tests can be very straightforward tests of the stated objectives, with no attempt to catch candidates out or to explore the boundaries of the syllabus. This is consistent with the intentions of many other current assessment initiatives to assess pupils on what they can do rather than on what they cannot. Indeed, it may be perfectly acceptable in some graded test schemes for candidates to know in advance what the questions will be, at any rate in outline. This applies, for example, to many components of the ABRSM music examinations. It is clear that success-orientation requires continual awareness by all concerned — test developers, teachers and pupils — that graded tests are essentially non-competitive, and that they are designed simply to demonstrate when candidates have achieved the specified levels of performance.

4.4 Curriculum-linking and curriculum reform

It would be quite wrong to assume that principles of criterion-referenced assessment and mastery learning are uppermost in the minds of teachers when they decide to adopt a graded test scheme, or when they are actually implementing it in the classroom. While they may support those principles, many teachers are much more interested in the curricular and/or pedagogical reforms intrinsic to the scheme. In fact, many graded test schemes can be regarded primarily as assessment-led curriculum development projects, which provide a vehicle for the relevant reform to take place. Whereas these reforms usually feature a move towards more pupil-centred learning, the precise nature of the reform varies according to the subject area, or even the individual scheme. For example, GOML schemes often involve a move away from traditional grammar-based courses, which include strong elements of writing and translation, towards syllabuses based on functions, notions and communication in authentic contexts. An example in which the reform is a pedagogical one is given by the Kent Mathematics Project, where individualized learning from workcards replaces class teaching.

It is important to recognize that the three key features of graded test schemes which were identified earlier are conceptually separate from these curricular reforms. Indeed the graded tests themselves may not be essential to such reform, but nevertheless the schemes are a catalyst for curricular change and act to support and consolidate its implementation in several ways. They provide benchmarks to assist with monitoring individual progress. They also provide a structure for teaching and learning which helps to define the classroom situation, both for teachers and for pupils. Finally, they give status to the reform in question.

There is case study evidence (Pennycuick and Murphy, 1988) that teacher enthusiasm for schemes is based at least as much on the prospect of achieving desired curricular and pedagogical reform as on graded test principles, and that the assessment structure has relatively low, although still significant, prominence in teacher and pupil perceptions of some schemes. Equally it is clear that graded test schemes have considerable potential for influencing or controlling curriculum development, either positively or negatively. In particular it may be noted that they tend to maintain existing subject boundaries. However, schemes rarely cover the whole curriculum for a given subject, and this factor limits their curriculum backwash effects.

4.5 Curricular and pedagogical issues

Level-progression in graded test schemes may be compared with Gagné's (1968) concept of learning hierarchies. However, the working parties which develop the schemes are likely to allocate objectives to levels as much on a pragmatic basis, using their experience, as by any logical analysis of which tasks are prerequisites for which other tasks. It may be noted that there are usually no age restrictions on entry for graded tests, although schemes may be aimed at specific target groups. There may in fact be considerable flexibility in the ways in which schemes are used by schools, for example in deciding which pupils take which levels, in the order of treatment within a level, in the structure of individual lessons, in the tasks assigned to individual pupils, or even in the way testing is organized. Difficulties in sequencing material may be created by the need to integrate graded test syllabuses with textbook courses. Some schemes, particularly in modern languages, draw a distinction between teaching syllabuses and testing syllabuses. The need for effective learning to include continual revision indicates that analysis of learning elements into a linear hierarchy cannot be the only factor in establishing a successful, teaching sequence.

In an assessment system which specifies clearly the tasks to be performed by candidates (the curriculum-linking feature) there may be a danger of learning by rote. The more precise the specification, the more candidates will know what the test questions will be, and be able to practise accordingly. Another factor which may encourage teachers to 'teach to the test' in graded test schemes is emphasis on success for the great majority of pupils (the success-orientation feature). In some circumstances this might not matter if the specified skills are in fact acquired. Indeed 'teaching to the test' is perhaps not very far from 'relating instruction and assessment closely to the objectives'. But it could still be argued that restriction of the curriculum to the test items themselves is undesirable. One reservation about GOML schemes in general is the possible use of testing syllabuses as teaching syllabuses. This might have consequent negative curricular backwash effects (e.g. excessive use of English), in addition to overemphasis on testing. Some teachers doubt whether schemes enable pupils to reach a point at which they begin to use language creatively.

In schemes where learning is individualized, again there is the danger of 'learning to the test', permitting apparent progress without genuine learning, and actual cheating on tests may also have this effect. Cheating may become a greater risk if different pupils take the same test at different times. But it would be a pity to overemphasize the possible negative effects of graded testing. There is evidence that schemes may be handled in such a way as to minimize such effects, and there are also significant positive backwash effects, for example the achievement of greater stress on oral or practical work.

4.6 Suitability across the ability range

The use of terms such as 'low-ability', 'mixed-ability' and 'ability range' (within a class or across an age cohort) is often related to the ways in which pupils are allocated to teaching groups. In practice, individual pupils' abilities are usually determined by their attainments, which are in most cases assessed by their perform-ance on some form of test. The concepts of ability and range of ability are norm-referenced, and it may be asked whether they are appropriate in the context of graded test schemes, which are not intended to discriminate between pupils by the measurement of individual differences.

In principle, provided the mastery level is reached, the actual graded test scores attained, and the rank order of candidates, are not important. But even if test scores are ignored it is still possible to use graded testing to define an ability range, by consideration of the levels reached and individual rates of progress from one level to the next. One possibility for differentiation between pupils at the same level is according to when they become ready to take the tests. 'More able' pupils may be defined as those who proceed faster and/or further through the levels, and it would therefore appear that the concept of ability range is still viable in the context of graded tests, even if it is no longer defined in terms of test scores.

However, the nature of ability is modified by graded test schemes in the sense that they assess different types of attainment than do more traditional approaches. For example, ability in writing may be replaced by an emphasis on oral ability or on practical ability. In some GOML schemes the multi-dimensional nature of ability is stressed by the requirement for separate standards to be achieved in reading, listening and speaking. In an individualized learning scheme, the ability to learn by listening to a teacher gives way to the ability to work independently and to learn from workcards. It may well be that individual children occupy different places on the 'ability range' as a result of these different emphases. Perhaps more significantly, many teachers regard the principles of graded testing to be consistent with a wish to play down individual differences in attainment between pupils. But there is no evidence that any significant changes in allocation systems have resulted from the introduction of graded tests.

A major policy issue for graded assessment is whether to design schemes for a wide or a limited ability range. One scheme which has opted for the latter is the School Science Certificate, whose target group is fourth and fifth formers who would not be entered for public examinations. In mathematics, the development of limited ability 'graduated' tests is recommended by the Cockcroft Report (DES, 1982b). Such schemes do provide an assessment system for less able pupils which has currency beyond the individual school, but there is a serious problem of the status of the schemes in the minds not only of the pupils themselves, but also of teachers, parents and employers. However, less able pupils who take part in full-ability schemes may become disillusioned by lack of visible progress over time, by repetition of content, and by comparison with the achievements of more able pupils (Brown, 1983). Even if schemes enable weak pupils to experience initial success, maintaining this is not easy.

It is clearly difficult to design common curriculum and assessment materials which both provide a challenge to more able pupils and offer a realistic chance of success to less able pupils. One advantage of limited-range schemes is that they can achieve an appropriate level of difficulty for their target groups. However, even limited-range schemes may be at a disadvantage for low-ability pupils in that they cannot cater for the possibility of a pupil doing more work at the same level of difficulty (thereby continuing to achieve success), rather than moving up the hierarchy of levels. Once tasks are defined in terms of levels, it may be difficult to convince pupils that progress is being made unless they move up the levels.

The desire to make a graded test scheme suitable across a wide ability range may limit its scope, leading to doubts about the scheme for the most able pupils. There may be concern about the transition to A-level courses, and there may be a need to supplement the scheme for able pupils. The pressures of the public examination system and the need for graded tests to lead to some form of national certification has led to the development of Mode 2 or 3 examinations linked to some schemes, requiring certain compromises to be made on graded test principles, but enabling the schemes to be followed by able fourth- and fifth-year pupils. The problems at the top end of the ability range appear less severe than those at the bottom end, but both appear to increase higher up the age range.

4.7 Pupil motivation

Enhanced pupil motivation is stated as a main aim by many graded test schemes, and success-orientation is one of the ways in which it is hoped that this will be achieved. Graded tests are planned to avoid the drawback of traditional examinations whereby many pupils experience a sense of failure both by being compared unfavourably with others and by being presented with tasks which are of an inappropriate level of difficulty. Graded test schemes are designed to provide a challenge while having a high pass rate, and success in the form of 'doing better than others' is replaced by success in 'acquiring skills' and 'passing tests'. As we have seen, this non-competitive form of assessment is not necessarily egalitarian, since some will progress faster and further than others.

It does seem necessary from motivational considerations that success should be valid in the sense that passing the graded test is seen to be synonymous with acquiring the tested skills. Otherwise pupil perception of success may be short-lived. Whether or not the scheme is certificated, it is important not only that the pupils should regard themselves as successful, but also that they should be regarded as successful by others such as teachers, peers and family. Success may be perceived during the tests (when pupils find they can do the tasks), or when pupils are told they have passed, or when certificates are presented, or when pupils receive praise (perhaps when they take certificates home). Motivation may be due partly to encouragement from past (actual) success, and partly to the stimulus of the prospect of future (hypothetical) success. Graded test schemes aim to provide frequent positive reinforcement of pupil motivation by means of short-term goals consisting of readily available targets. The idea that success and motivation can be mutually reinforcing is fundamental to graded assessment philosophy. However, the intended emphasis on success is not necessarily realized in practice, and it may be more difficult for graded test schemes to continue the enablement of pupil success than to provide the initial experience.

In the long term there is the question of what will happen if graded tests are extended to more levels and more subjects. Intrinsic motivational factors may become more significant than extrinsic factors such as certificates. However, in all three schemes studied by Pennycuick (1986), pupils expressed support for the testing structures, and for the style, content and difficulty level of the tests, and this support extended to some pupils who said they do not normally like tests. The graded tests do act as an incentive for pupils, although older pupils feel that what really matter are public examinations. These act as a major motivating factor by giving national certification, which provides qualifications for further education and enhances employment prospects.

A further possible factor is extra commitment and enthusiasm on the part of teachers, particularly those who have been involved in the working parties developing the schemes, with an associated sense of purpose and of control over the development. If teacher enthusiasm is important in motivating pupils, large-scale schemes developed by examination boards might not necessarily be as successful as those developed locally by groups of teachers. A parallel point is made by Nuttall and Goldstein (1984) who suggest that the *graded* part of graded testing may be relatively insignificant, and that a modular scheme might serve as well. There is case study evidence that pupils are motivated by teachers who make the work interesting, but little to suggest that teacher enthusiasm as a pupil motivator is more important in the graded test context than it is in any other form of teaching.

It was suggested earlier that enthusiasm may be based more on associated curricular reforms than on graded test principles. If the particular syllabus objectives and teaching methods adopted by a scheme are predominant as a motivating factor, new graded test schemes might not necessarily be as successful as existing schemes, unless they are also founded on perceived curricular needs. A good example of such needs is given by the communicative approach to language learning. Pupils like the stress on authentic oral communication which they perceive to be practical, useful and relevant. They enjoy the work partly because they can succeed, but also because they regard the objective of realistic interaction with native speakers to be a valid one. This extends to enjoyment of the actual testing process, and can be reinforced by a genuine sense of achievement on using the language, say on a day trip to France, although this is only a possibility in some areas. Clearly the style of assessment is important from a motivational point of view, as well as the curriculum content and the style of teaching. Another positive factor may be that assessment objectives are clearly defined so that pupils know more precisely what they are expected to do.

But there are also negative effects. Pupils can become bored by overemphasis on testing, particularly if the same topics arise in consecutive levels. Where testing is conducted on an individual basis, waiting for other pupils to be tested can create discipline problems in addition to the difficulty that no actual teaching can take place during that time. There may also be demotivating factors in schemes where learning is individualized – loss of continuity, lack of perceived relevance, difficulty in understanding the workcards, or possible abuse of the system. In all schemes motivation may be a function of length of involvement with the scheme. In new schemes there may be Hawthorne or other initial effects, although established schemes are still novel to each succeeding age cohort of pupils.

A final possible factor to be considered is that of competition (or its absence). Many pupils do not see themselves as competing with their peers in the sense of striving to excel them, and would not wish to do so, but equally there is a strong desire not to be left behind. Pupils are motivated to keep up with their fellows, but competition is rather against targets and standards set by the scheme. Indeed, graded tests seem appropriate for a classroom atmosphere in which competition among pupils is discouraged.

No clear picture emerges of what the key motivating factors are, or of the extent to which any improved motivation is a permanent effect. Different pupils are motivated by different factors and combinations of factors, and individuals may react differently in different contexts. The possible results of improved motivation, when it occurs, are that pupils will become more amenable as a result of improved attitudes created by enjoyment and/or satisfaction from achievement and/or perceived relevance of their graded test course. This may lead to several effects, notably better behaviour and greater effort, hopefully reflected in improved performance.

Not all teachers are convinced of the disciplinary benefits. For example, an oral approach to language teaching can make lessons more difficult to control. Indeed, it may be that discipline must in the first place be such as to permit operation of the scheme! Perhaps the conclusions for teachers are simply not to be overly sanguine about motivational benefits of graded test schemes, and to adopt a heuristic approach to their operation of the schemes with individual groups of pupils in order to maximize potential benefits, while remembering that there are reasons other than purely motivational ones for the development and use of graded tests, for example to provide a vehicle for curriculum reform, or to provide a clear description of pupil attainment.

4.8 Teacher perspectives

Graded test schemes permit flexibility in the ways in which they may be used by participating schools, and there are significant variations in practice. Department heads and subject teachers take account of several factors in determining the place of the graded test scheme within the course structure. These factors vary among schools and among schemes, but may include timetabling and setting considerations, resource constraints, and the pressures of external examinations. If the graded test scheme does not provide the entire course it is necessary to mesh work towards the scheme with other work in the subject, with topic selection and sequencing decisions being strongly influenced by the progression of levels. The 'ability' of the pupils and the logistics of testing are other factors affecting decisions about how each teaching group is involved with the scheme.

The temporal organization of the schools, where timetable

changes and automatic promotion occur at yearly intervals, poses some difficulties for graded testing, in which levels are not designed for a fixed time allocation, but where the intention is that pupils are entered for tests when they are ready. Even in individualized learning schemes there is a tendency to encourage pupils to achieve 'completion' in some sense by the end of the academic year. The principle of readiness is inhibited by the imposition of deadlines, whether the scheme is individualized or based on class teaching. In the latter case, teachers are likely to find it difficult to cope with groups working at different levels, or different stages of the same level. Vertical timetabling may provide at least a partial solution to problems created by the year-group structure of schools (the 'lock-step' system). However, mixed-age classes may only be operable on the basis of modular curricular organization, which again is likely to require fixed time slots, although if this were done on a termly basis it might become easier for pupils to transfer to a higher level group when ready, or to stay at the same level if not.

The logistics of test administration is a major concern. External administration (e.g. candidate entry, issue of certificates) is a concern for those running the scheme rather than teachers in the schools. It is the internal administration of the tests which creates difficulties for the latter. One is the increase in teacher workload resulting from individualized assessment. Application of the principle of readiness is another. A third problem is the time spent by teachers on testing as opposed to teaching, perhaps leading to boredom and/or reduced pupil progress. Finally, there are disciplinary difficulties (e.g. preventing cheating, occupying the rest of the class during oral testing, controlling remedial groups taking practical science tests).

Several possible solutions to these difficulties may be considered. One is to conduct individual testing during lunchtimes, but this would increase workload still further, and does not appear to be realistic in the long term. Another solution would be, if resources were to become available, a reduction in group size or the provision of cover for teachers involved in testing. The availability of a second teacher would reduce or eliminate all the above difficulties, and some teachers feel that such cover would be the only fully satisfactory solution. Failing that, a third possibility is to reduce the volume of testing by simplifying procedures, reverting to a greater proportion of group assessment, or bypassing levels. It clearly helps if graded tests are seen as a *replacement* for existing school examinations and assessment procedures.

It is not only the logistics of testing which can create an overall increase in teacher workload. Teachers may find periods to be harder work and more exhausting than more traditional teaching. Extra work may be required to integrate scheme and textbook materials into a coherent course. Record keeping to monitor individual progress leads to an increased load. Workload effects on staff are cumulative, depending on the number of classes involved in the scheme. Teachers may be reluctant to extend a scheme to more groups, in order to restrict increased strain to tolerable levels.

The introduction of graded tests appears to require some increased resources in terms of accommodation and materials, and may also pose resource management problems. Case study evidence suggests that the availability of adequate resources is a significant factor in the viability of schemes. These include the provision of textbooks and/or workcards, equipment and consumable materials, and satisfactory acoustics for oral work. Schemes are likely to be funded largely from existing budget allocations, both within the schools and within the LEAs concerned. It is clear that there are substantial hidden costs of LEA-based schemes which have to be absorbed. These may include major time commitments by advisory staff, secondment of teachers, costs of working party and in-service training meetings, secretarial costs and the costs of materials of various kinds (e.g. circulars, test materials, certificates). In general, the benefits to the LEAs are non-quantifiable (e.g. pupil motivation, curriculum development, staff in-service training, prestige). The need for in-service training is stressed by Newbould and Massey (1984), Harrison (1985) and Rutherford (1979). Rutherford, writing in the wider context of criterion-referenced programmes, states:

> We have found that the problems with locally designed criterion-referenced curricula neither seem to be rooted in the basic concepts and approaches of such curricula, nor in the specific content of the materials which have been developed, rather the problem seems to lie in the fact that school-built programmes, and commercial programmes as well, do not develop a support system to accompany the content structure system. (Rutherford, 1979, p.48)

LEA advisers play a key role in such support systems for the schemes studied by Pennycuick (1986). In-service support falls into three main categories: (i) written materials in the form of teachers' guides or circulars, (ii) meetings, workshops or courses, and (iii) advisory visits to schools. It appears that the main need for further training felt by teachers is in the style of teaching and testing, not in the principles or administration of the scheme.

It may be supposed that the rewards accruing to individual teachers vary at least in part according to their depth of involvement, and their perceptions of the scheme. Harrison (1985) argues that 'the involvement of teachers in curriculum development improves morale and commitment'. This may extend to all participating teachers, but may be particularly valid for working party members, who are likely to have a strong sense of ownership of the scheme as a result of helping to devise the syllabuses and tests, and therefore a personal stake in its successful operation and dissemination. Teachers who have not been members of the working parties may nevertheless have sufficient commitment to the curriculum and assessment principles behind the scheme for this to compensate for any perceived loss of freedom to plan and develop their own courses, or they may welcome the graded test structure as an aid to curriculum planning.

Even if the scheme is found difficult to operate, staff may persevere since they see advantages for their pupils and perhaps for their own self-esteem. Increased workload is a potential, but not necessarily an actual, staff demotivator since teachers may feel that the scheme is worth the effort in terms of results. Staff morale and enthusiasm may be encouraged by a sense of satisfaction in pupil achievement even if teachers do not particularly enjoy the periods, and may experience a feeling of loss of control during them. A very positive factor is that graded test schemes appear to encourage unanimity of approach and hence departmental unity. Teachers who have adopted a scheme voluntarily are likely to emphasize its beneficial features in their own minds even if they also stress its problems to a researcher. There is the possibility that they may use the scheme as a means of obtaining more resources or recognition. Heads of department in particular may perceive a graded test scheme as a source of departmental prestige by drawing attention to their modernity and commitment, and even as an outlet for ambition. All teachers may experience a sense of pride from their developed expertise in the efficient administration and successful operation of the scheme. However, the overall impression from case study research (Pennycuick, 1986) is that the overriding reason for teacher support of graded test schemes is that they feel that these schemes benefit the pupils more than whatever they have replaced.

4.9 Certificates

Most graded test schemes issue certificates which attempt to describe in detail what it is that successful candidates can do. There are several problems inherent in such certificate descriptions. One is that no guarantee can be given as to the extent to which mastery is retained. Secondly, at higher levels, it is not clear whether a certificate holder may also be assumed to be a master of all preceding levels. Thirdly, many schemes base their performance standards on some form of aggregate score, which leads to loss of information concerning individual performance on the tests. There are likely to be skills listed on the certificates awarded to successful candidates which have not in fact been attained.

In practice most candidates may score far more that the minimum required level, but there is no way of indicating this on the certificate, and for a pupil who has only scraped through there is no way of telling whether some skills have been well performed in the test and others not at all, or whether all skills have been performed in a mediocre way. But it may be pointed out that whatever the problems of graded test certificate descriptions they do represent an advance on public examinations in which results are presented merely as a single grade, in terms of providing users with information that is both meaningful and manageable.

There is a tension between the simultaneous requirements for certificate descriptions to be both precise and concise. This creates a further problem, of the level of specificity required in individual skill descriptions. There may be a lack of clarity in what is meant by a particular description in terms of difficulty, assumed knowledge or context. It is doubtful whether skills can satisfactorily be defined in such a way as to be context-free; this interesting issue is discussed further by Murphy and Pennycuick (1986) and by Nuttall and Goldstein (1984). Whether the validity of certificate descriptions should perhaps be of greater concern is related to another issue, the use that is actually made of graded test certificates by pupils and others, and this will now be considered.

The skill descriptions on the reverse side of certificates may have some role in enhancing the status of these certificates by providing evidence that holders have acquired genuine and worthwhile skills, and that a serious process of assessment has been carried out before certificates are awarded. However, it might be felt that the statements of achievement on the obverse of the certificates, and particularly the appearance of county crests and signatures of directors of education, are more significant for status and hence motivation than are the detailed descriptions of skills attained. Certainly if pupils display certificates at home it will be the obverse sides that are on show.

The identity of the main intended audiences for the skill descriptions is not clear. The language used is often inappropriate for the pupils themselves to understand or to relate to the tasks they have done. However, for teachers the lists of skills not only perform the function of defining objectives, but also may be used to assist in the formative assessment processes of monitoring pupil progress and diagnosis of individual difficulties. A further possible function of graded test certificates is to provide employers or selectors with accurate information on what holders can do, and it is perhaps here that validity problems become most significant. However, employers are used to dealing with national examination results which do not include descriptions of skills acquired, and although in principle they may favour a move in that direction, it would probably be necessary to make them more aware of graded test schemes and convince them of the value of the associated certificates. Business studies is one area in which graded test certificates already appear to enhance employment prospects.

4.10 A note on reliability

Traditional test theory is not appropriate for the study of graded tests. In particular, 'reliability coefficients' require variance in test scores, which is against the spirit of non-competitive tests. Nevertheless, there are two aspects of reliability which are relevant here: consistency of marking and consistency of the conditions of test administration.

In many graded test schemes, testing and marking are conducted by the candidate's own teacher, subject to specified conditions. Clearly, reliability of marking is dependent on the experience, commitment, expertise and training of the teacher and, as Harrison (1982) points out, 'examiner judgement is a perennial problem in all task-oriented tests unless the marking is done entirely objectively'. However, the case study research reported by Pennycuick (1986) found no evidence that marking by teachers is seen as a significant source of unreliability.

As Nuttall and Goldstein (1984) suggest, variation in test conditions may be a more salient source of unreliability. Such variation may arise from several factors:

1 Whether the test is concentrated in one session or held over several.
2 The physical conditions of the test.
3 The degree of permissible assistance to the pupil during the test.
4 Opportunities for pupils to cheat.
5 Opportunities for pupils to re-take parts of the test after failure.

It seems desirable from the point of view of perceived fairness that schemes should define conditions for test administration which cover these factors.

However, it could also be argued that greater specification of the conditions for test administration, although it might enhance reliability, would restrict the freedom of teachers to operate a scheme in the way they feel to be most suitable for the particular conditions in individual participating schools. One point that could be made is that if fairness is the reason for emphasis on test reliability, then other considerations should also be taken into account, for example available resources, the extent to which pupils are given specific test preparation, and the extent to which they are ready for tests (both cognitively and attitudinally).

Secondly, the importance of reliability is dependent on the use to be made of test results, and in particular whether graded tests are seen as high-quality teacher-made tests for internal assessment purposes or as an alternative to external examinations. Many of those involved with graded test schemes are far more concerned with the effects of the tests on classroom practice than they are with technical aspects of the tests, and may prefer to deal with any consequences of unreliability rather than to tackle its sources. Nevertheless, it does seem necessary for public confidence in the schemes that the tests are seen to be fair, and it may be argued that reliability becomes more important if assessment is terminal than if the pupil is continuing to higher levels of the scheme.

4.11 Conclusion

In conclusion, the following points should be borne in mind in any discussion of graded tests. First, although graded test schemes share the key features of level-progression, success-orientation and curriculum-linking identified above, they also exhibit considerable diversity. Secondly, many schemes are closely associated with curricular and/or pedagogical reform. Thirdly, graded tests serve a range of assessment functions. Since they are not designed to discriminate between candidates, they are essentially non-competitive within each level. Fourthly, it may not always be easy to apply graded test principles in practice; the operation of schemes in schools is subject to pragmatic considerations.

A particular issue which remains unresolved is whether schemes are best designed for a wide or a restricted ability range. The long-term motivational effects of graded tests are not clear, and there are technical problems (e.g. in the description of pupil achievement) which may continue to be troublesome. However, graded tests represent a significant component of the recent surge of assessment initiatives, and deserve further evaluation. Their relationship to other initiatives, in particular GCSE, has not been tackled in this chapter, but will be taken up in Chapter 6. It can certainly be argued that many of the aims of GCSE might be better served by a system of graded tests rather than by an examination system offering a range of grades on a fixed date.

Chapter 5

Modular and Unit Credit Systems

Henry Macintosh

5.1 Introduction

As is so often the case with educational buzz words, modules, units or credits (the terms are for practical purposes inter-changeable) are not something new, although their use within the secondary curriculum in Britain on any scale has only occurred in the past 5 years. It is interesting to note incidentally that the first major proposal in 1977 to use a unit credit system in Britain was rejected as being too radical a departure from existing practice and as requiring considerable organizational changes (The Munn Report, SED, 1977).

The current interest in modules (the term that will be used here) stems largely from a concern about how to manage learning most effectively in the interests of all students. One way of tackling this problem is to replace the 1- or 2-year courses currently so prevalent within our examination dominated secondary curriculum by smaller units of learning or modules. The supporters of modules claim a number of benefits for students, teachers and curricula, particularly in relation to enhanced motivation and cross-curricula developments. Others, however, point to the lack of curriculum coherence and the resource and management problems that can result from their widespread use. There is as yet insufficient evidence based on tested practice to set out a realistic 'for and against' balance sheet, not least because something which in the early stages of a new development looks to be a disadvantage or even a threat can turn out in time to be an asset. A good example of this is the greater accountability for both teachers and pupils which can result from the use of short-term learning objectives.

A major worry about the present enthusiasm for modules is the rather simplistic nature of much of the discussion about their use and the consequential belief that there are absolute answers to such questions as 'How long is a module?' or that there is such a thing as modular assessment. The length of a learning unit must always depend upon the proposed outcomes, the nature of subject matter and the needs, interests and abilities of the students tempered by practical considerations of manageability and resources (see, e.g. SCRE, 1984). As far as assessment is concerned what is needed are not new techniques but the will to use the full range that already exists and to use them at the most appropriate time in order to generate relevant evidence regarding performance. The basic problem is thus attitudinal and not technical. Styles of teaching and methods of assessment must vary both within and between modules if they are to mesh with and reflect the variety of intentions within any curriculum. It is not, therefore, sensible to introduce modules without first analysing the nature of the curriculum one wishes to deliver and how one wishes to deliver it.

The continued existence of formal public examinations in Britain for most students at age 16 has also caused two quite distinct issues – assessment and certification – to become entangled. Much of the current debate about modular assessment is in reality about modular certification, whether this be for the GCSE with its national criteria or for A level, or to meet the requirements of bodies like the Business and Technician Education Council, City and Guilds of London Institute and the Royal Society of Arts. In order to consider the significant assessment issues in relation to modules it is important therefore to avoid getting bogged down in the details of current certification and to concentrate instead upon the 14–18 curriculum, since this is where the main thrust for modules is presently coming. The Technical and Vocational Education Initiative (TVEI) extension proposals have been particularly influential here. In broad terms one is seeing a shift towards a curriculum which stresses skills and concepts at the expense of content, which lessens the emphasis placed upon single subjects, extends the range of evidence upon which judgements are based, stresses student autonomy and makes use of recording systems which encourage formative diagnostic usage. It is thus essentially a curriculum designed to promote equity through enhancing the potential of all young people.

5.2 Whole-course planning

In order to deliver this kind of agenda, assessment must become an integral part of whole-course and ultimately of whole-curriculum planning, built in from the outset and not bolted on as an afterthought. This must occur whatever the size or length of the course. It is important moreover to recognize that a teaching module is not necessarily the same as an assessment module. The extent to which the two match will depend upon the intentions of the course as a whole and upon the points at which it seems most useful to appraise and discuss student performance collectively or individually. This could occur in the middle of a module or require assessment which runs over several modules.

Whole-course planning requires three questions to be asked and answered:

1 What are the intended outcomes of the course?
2 What evidence will be needed/can be provided in order to establish that learning relevant to these outcomes has occurred?
3 What teaching/learning activities will need to be provided in order to produce that evidence?

The outcomes referred to in the first question may, of course, derive from different sources. Some, like the GCSE criteria, will be laid down externally. Others will result from negotiation and discussion between teachers and students. Effective feedback, particularly in relation to short-term goals is, however, more likely to result from openness and sharing in relation to both outcomes and methods of assessment. Currently, the range of evidence regarded as appropriate for assessment purposes, particularly in public examinations, is extremely impoverished. One has only to look at the variety of forms which written evidence can take, e.g. reports, diaries, logbooks, stories, questionnaires, letters, notes, drafts and radio and TV scripts, and compare these with the range which students are actually asked to produce in order to appreciate the extent of the mismatch. Even more telling is the stress laid upon writing at the expense of other forms of communication. Of course it is important when extending the range of evidence not to over-assess, particularly when, as with modular developments, there is likely to be a significant increase in the use of 'in-course' assessment and in the numbers of those involved in the assessment process. However, over-assessment can be avoided by greater emphasis upon whole-institutional and whole-curriculum planning and by always asking the question, what is the minimum evidence needed in order to make sensible and fair statements about performance?

The third question is the most problematic of the three. It assumes, as indeed do all three questions, a view of the curriculum which is assessment led – a view strongly supported by current government policies. It is thus predicated upon the notion that if the assessment matches the outcomes then pedagogy will also change to provide a three-way match. Unfortunately, the evidence of curriculum projects such as the Schools History Project which have put a high investment into changing assessment suggests that changes in pedagogy lag substantially behind those in assessment (Williams, 1986). It may be that modules with their potential for widening the range of evidence and their stress upon short-term objectives can improve this situation. It may be that less emphasis upon formal written examinations and greater stress upon in-course assessment will also help, but we have no right to assume that this will automatically be the case. The heart of the problem lies in our current lack of knowledge about how students actually learn within particular areas of the curriculum. This means that the proposed outcomes may well not match, or may be sequenced in ways which do not match, the realities of learning. It is thus essential that future pre- and in-service programmes address these issues in practical terms.

If one wishes to enhance feedback, three general issues in relation to assessment are particularly significant, namely Criterion-referencing, Progression and Credit Transfer. None of the three, with the possible exception of Credit Transfer, is unique to modular developments, as other chapters in this book have underlined. All have, however, significant implications for the design of assessment programmes which will secure both coherence and quality – features which are absolutely crucial to an increased use of modules.

5.3 Criterion-referencing

As with modules there is nothing new about criterion-referencing. There has been, however, in Britain as in many other countries a significant shift in recent years away from models of assessment which compare an individual's performance with those of other individuals (norm-referencing) to models which reference the performance of all individuals against specified criteria (criterion-referencing). Too much can be made of this distinction and in practical terms the assessment of individuals will continue to be a mixture of both, as well as taking on board the possibility of referencing individuals against their own past performance. The shift, and it is only a shift, is none the less extremely significant because it renders the notion of the normal curve of distribution wholly inappropriate as a basis upon which to construct assessment. Assessment both in terms of 'setting' and 'marking' is instead required to deliver in practical terms the theoretical notion that all criteria are accessible to all students even though the extent to which they meet them will vary at any given point in time. Unless ways are found of doing this it will be extremely difficult to measure individual progress and to make positive diagnostic use of the information gained from assessment. This will mean that many of the questioning techniques in current use in examinations and in classrooms, designed primarily to discriminate between candidates, and the ways in which they are marked, are no longer appropriate. It will also be necessary to review many of the ground rules upon which public examinations are currently run: unwillingness to supply mark schemes to all teachers, reluctance to involve teachers in the assessment of their own students and the use of substantial numbers of lettered grades to name but three.

5.4 Positive assessment

It is all very well to be dismissive about current questioning and marking techniques, but what in real terms does positive or differentiated assessment (the terms in current use to describe the change) mean and what does such assessment look like? Very simply it means that any question (and this is shorthand for problem, enquiry, etc.) must enable all those for whom it is intended to show, through their answers/solutions, what they can do in their own terms and be rewarded appropriately for showing it. (The phrase 'all those for whom it is intended' is absolutely crucial. In GCSE, for example, it will mean 90% of the ability range.) There are only really two ways of doing this: one is to ask everyone the same questions and the other is by asking different people different questions. In the first case, the weight of differentiation lies with the answers, while in the second it lies with the questions.

Differentiation through targeted questions of the kind referred to in the preceding paragraph implies some form of graded or laddered approach. In Chapter 4, Pennycuick addresses the principal issues involved in the construction and use of such tests. Three brief further points are, however, relevant in this context. First, if one relates specific questions to specific grades as a means of securing differentiation in, say, an examination like the GCSE, then the only grade that can be awarded is the one at which the questions are targetted. Safety nets, which allow lower grades to be awarded for bad performances on a higher grade paper or questions or vice versa, must be ruled out since they will inevitably dilute the degree of differentiation. Secondly, if graded tests are to be used to secure differentiation then it will be necessary to be much clearer than is currently the case about what constitutes mastery in terms of particular levels of performance. This is particularly important when modules are being used, since a graduated approach to differentiation will only work with modular programmes in which there is a clear progression from one module to another in terms of content, concepts or skills. Progression here means successful completion of whatever is required in the preceding module and this of course implies a hierarchy of learning tasks which are far from easy to develop. Thirdly, there is a real need to investigate the possibilities of graded coursework assignments as an alternative to the formal oral or written testing which forms the bulk of most existing graded test programmes.

The construction and marking of common questions for a wide ability range poses different but equally significant problems for the design of positive assessment schemes, not least because the bulk of current marking and setting techniques will not work. It is, moreover, not possible to get over this problem by setting a series of questions or part questions which get progressively more difficult. There is no difference except in degree in exposing students to part questions or part papers which they cannot answer than in exposing them to whole questions or whole papers.

The experience of projects like the Schools Council History Project, has suggested a number of strategies for achieving differentiation over a wide ability range by means of common questions of which the following would seem to be particularly important.

1   The creation of questions whose difficulty lies primarily in the tasks they set and not in their texts. This is essentially a counsel of perfection since the choice of text will depend upon both subject and context. There is also the question of necessary technical vocabulary where failure to understand will quite rightly inhibit the capacity to respond. There will also be occasions where what is being tested and the forms taken by the questions are so inextricably linked that if you do not understand the one you cannot answer the other. Despite all these difficulties there is an enormous amount that can be done to improve the accessibility of the questions asked in both examination and classroom.

2   The inappropriateness of questions that test factual recall as an end in itself or which can only be marked on a right/wrong basis. This rules out the use of short answer questions and objective items.

3   The construction of questions which pose problems or

dilemmas which can be unpacked or unpeeled in different ways by different students and answered at different levels. Such questions must aim to test a range of skills and not be targetted at single skills (an impossibility in practical terms in any case).

4 The abandonment of mark schemes based on the notion of correct or model answers and their replacement by schemes based upon levels of response. A top-down model for marking which inhibits feedback is thus replaced by a bottom-up model which facilitates it.

Despite the very real practical difficulties in constructing questions and mark schemes along these lines there is now considerable evidence from the Schools Council History Project to show that it can be done and that they will work over a wide ability range. There is also a need to match work on written questions with parallel work on oral questions and upon coursework assignments or case studies. The latter indeed may well turn out to be by far the best way of securing differentiation through common tasks. It is no use, however, changing the kinds of questions asked, the problems posed or the assignments set in public examinations if norm-referenced assessment and the normal curve of distribution continue to dominate classroom practice – and this, as has already been pointed out, is as much a matter of attitude as it is of technique.

5.5 Progression

The term progression – like modules, much in vogue – is currently used in two quite distinct although connected ways. To some it simply means recognizing progress and is hence concerned with issues relating to defining, measuring and recording individual progress. To others it is concerned with facilitating progress, smoothing out the passage between different courses of study, and it stresses therefore progress into and out of particular courses of study and ways of achieving this through enhancement or exemption. In subject terms the American Advanced Placement Program administered by Educational Testing Service (ETS) on behalf of the College Board is probably the best example of this approach to exemption, enabling students as it does to gain up to 2 years advanced standing at universities across the United States. Exemption is a particularly significant issue at the present time in England and Wales given the multiplicity of certificating agencies and the ever-increasing costs of taking the examinations through which certification is gained. It will, therefore, be particularly interesting to see how the National Council for Vocational

Qualifications (NCVQ) tackles this issue as a possible first step towards establishing some form of national credit system involving all institutions and all examinations.

Modules both hinder and help progression. Modules can encourage cross-curricular developments through courses based upon themes and experiences. But unlike subject work, of which there is in any case much greater familiarity, such courses are horizontal rather than vertical in terms of their development. As such they present very real problems for the recording of progress under arrangements which are designed essentially for subject-based vertical progression. On the other hand, modules can help progression in terms of exemption by making it easier to identify specific requirements within units which form a part of larger courses. There are, however, real risks that such courses will lack overall cohesion and this underlines the need for developing a management framework for modular curricula. In particular it is important to ensure that all courses of study for all students can demonstrate:

1 Clear connections between what has gone before and what is available in the future.
2 A continuous relationship between process and content.
3 A consistent relationship between learning programmes and assessment criteria.
4 The need and the opportunities for cooperation and inter-action between individuals and, where relevant, between subjects and between institutions.

Frameworks along these lines must ultimately form the basis for whole-institutional and whole-curriculum planning of which modules will constitute a part if progression in the broadest sense of the term is to be furthered without loss of quality or coherence.

5.6 Credit transfer

Credit transfer is the process whereby qualifications and/or learning experiences are given recognition or credit such as will enable students who possess the one or who have undergone the other to progress to the next stage whatever this may be. There are three basic ways in which any system of credit transfer can operate:

1 The recognition of alternative qualifications for initial entry into courses of study.
2 The granting of exemption from parts of courses to students with suitable and identifiable previous experience.

3 The introduction and development of study schemes based specifically on the principles of cumulative and transferable credit.

The implications of credit transfer for course design and/or assessment in the way in which it is undertaken and described depends very much upon whether the prime concern is admission or exemption. If it is the former then the need to analyse and describe what has actually happened in gaining the qualification or certificate, while interesting and useful, is not essential. If the latter then it is absolutely crucial. In consequence, an examination such as A-level with its results described in global whole-course grades can be used for admission purposes (although it is a poor predictor) but not for establishing exemption.

One of the attractions of modules is their potential for accumulating credit over time, banking it and then cashing it in, when and where appropriate. A number of large schemes have been set up to address these issues and provide a service to institutions, notably the Northern Partnership for Records of Achievement Unit Accreditation Scheme, the Oxfordshire Examinations Syndicate Credit Bank (which despite its name is not an examining board but a group of schools) and the Cambridge Syndicate's A-level and A/S Module Bank. The problems facing these and other similar schemes do not lie primarily in the building up of credit, still less in the banking process, although these both require careful thought and preparation. They lie essentially in 'cashing in', which means turning completed units or courses into certificates issued by approved bodies. It is hardly surprising, therefore, that the Northern Examining Authority regards the bringing together of its unit credit scheme, its record of achievement and its GCSE modules as its most pressing current problem.

Essentially the problem is one of aggregation and hence of working out equitable and justifiable rules of combination. The complexity of these rules will depend largely upon the methods used by the certificating body to describe performance. In the case of most school examinations these are lettered grades, currently six for A-level and A/S and seven for GCSE; numbers which do not fit easily alongside a shift towards criterion referencing. Given this situation, it will almost certainly be necessary, as the Associated Examining Board's (AEB) work with the Somerset LEA has shown, to introduce levels or grades within the assessment of the modules. These can then be combined in accordance with an agreed set of rules and turned into in this case GCSE grades.

The NEA and AEB proposals, although extremely carefully worked out, have a number of disadvantages which stem from the requirement to fit curriculum and assessment developments into a certificating system which was never designed to accommodate them or to facilitate criterion-referencing, progression and credit transfer. They impose a degree of conformity upon course structures which need flexibility, albeit carefully managed, if they are to deliver in a coherent fashion all the 14–18 agenda referred to earlier. They also tend to encourage the continuing use of moderation systems based upon oversight of detail rather than the achievement of quality control through agreement about procedural arrangements and their rigorous delivery. Some of these difficulties can be reduced as both teacher and examining agencies gain in confidence and experience and as appropriate in-service provision is developed to meet the very wide range of training needs required to further modular developments. These steps will not, however, be sufficient of themselves.

5.7 The future

What likelihood is there that significant changes can take place over the next few years in existing arrangements for grading and certification in public examinations, and what form might these take? Current government policies on both curriculum and examinations/assessment are a curious mixture of innovation and conservatism which, when taken together, make it difficult to discern any overall strategy. Developments like Records of Achievement and the GCSE criteria, which are bound to involve teachers directly in the assessment of their own students, lie alongside an enduring suspicion of coursework and teacher assessment. The encouragement of cross-curricula initiatives and integration in areas like Technology and Science for All, and through stress upon equal opportunities, co-exist with increasing emphasis upon subjects in both the primary and secondary curriculum. The proposals for a national curriculum with its break point at 16 and the continued existence of A-level seems at odds with the TVEI extension and emphasis upon a 14–18 curriculum which will meet the needs of all students and its break point at 14. It is clear that any resolution of these inconsistencies (assuming that they are seen as such) will take time. It is equally clear that unless changes do take place then our capacity to improve the quality of educational provision for all students will be severely inhibited. Shortage of resources, the ways in which teachers are trained, uncertainty about the working of the new Grant-related In-service Training programme (GRIST) and above all the continuing difficulties over teachers' remuneration and conditions of service, all further underline the point that real changes to the ways in which we assess, grade and certificate young people will be a slow process. The great merit of modules is that they have shown that both the possibilities and the need for change are much greater than many realize.

One way forward would seem to lie in greater use of curriculum profiling. By this is meant the provision of information about the formal curriculum which will enhance, supplement or complement information which is available through more formal examination assessment. This is one of the four main purposes recognized by the DES in its policy statement upon Records of Achievement but it has tended to take a back seat in many current developments. It is, however, an established feature of the provision made by many Further Education examining boards for certification and is also a key part of the Dorset Records of Achievement pilot project which aims to record performance over a student's complete curriculum.

One of the major problems facing achievement testing based upon criteria of the kind used in GCSE, however innovative that assessment, is that they contain elements, particularly process skills and group work, which are not amenable to formal testing and grading. It is also clear that work on learning pathways which must underpin any effective and workable system of criterion-referencing, particularly within subjects, is inhibited by the need to use for grading purposes frameworks of skills and concepts which are hierarchical rather than developmental in nature. These problems would be alleviated by the use of profiles which described what had occurred rather than judged it. If this were done much more effective and innovative use could be made of coursework programmes, particularly those which crossed subject boundaries. Such an approach could make use of the great amount of work currently underway in schools on profiling outside the formal curriculum. It would also serve to provide a single focus for in-service training in relation to assessment which is often wastefully fragmented between the requirements of schools and those of outside agencies conducting a range of competing examinations. Such a focus would not only raise significantly the level of experience but also enhance public confidence in teacher assessment. The degree to which this occurred would be a key factor in determining the pace of change itself.

There is, of course, a real risk in running school-based descriptive profiling alongside nationally validated, graded, formal assessment that the former will lack credibility, will be accorded low status and will not be used by the outside world. This is much less likely to happen where the information from the profile is directly related to that provided by the formal assessment. It is also less likely to occur at the present time in view of the growing interest in and use by employers of supplementary information about student achievement. There are also encouraging signs that some institutions of higher education wish to use supplementary information about academic performance as well as about extra-mural activities and personal characteristics (Stevens, 1987). Moreover, it is perfectly possible for the profiling component to form an integral part of an overall nationally agreed assessment package and to be accorded a weighting which reflects the existing degree of public confidence. Work currently underway between the Somerset LEA and the AEB on a Modular A-level programme provides a good illustration of the kind of lines upon which such a development might take place. A-level cores have been developed initially in the sciences which have a weighting of 60% together with a number of satellite modules each of which carry a weighting of 10% and four of which have to be taken by every student. These modules can extend or enhance the particular core with which they have been developed or can provide links with other cores. They can also provide different contexts for learning, e.g. the work-place. The core could easily constitute the graded part of the examination with the modules being profiled with performance in relation to them being either described or judged on a can do/cannot do basis (neither of which incidentally is as simple as this description suggests).

5.8 Conclusion

In practical terms it is much more likely that curriculum profiling if introduced on the lines suggested would form part of the assessment provision of a particular examination such as GCSE, A/S or A-level – offering more information about achievement on specific aspects of specific courses. It would, however, make much more sense to see profiling in its broadest sense as the hub of an overall assessment package for the 14–18 curriculum and ulti-mately as the basis for a 5–19 accreditation system. As already indicated, given present resources, attitudes and vested interests, this is only likely to come about (if at all) over a long-time scale, although the levels currently being developed for vocational qualifications by the NCVQ provide a possible model for the future. What is needed, however, in the shorter run is much more work upon both curriculum management and upon the develop-ment of whole-course programmes which integrate outcomes, assessment methods, evidence and learning strategies. In the construction of such programmes and in the resolution of management issues modules have a significant part to play, but not if they are seen as a solution to all our current problems.

Chapter 6

Facing the Change

6.1 The directions of change

In the preceding chapters we have reviewed some pioneering research and development work in the field of educational assessment, which has led in many cases to new initiatives in school-based assessment. All of this is much more than a set of abstract ideas or idealistic proposals as much of the work in profiling, graded tests and modular assessment has been observed as it was actually occurring in schools around the country. In one sense what we have presented has been selected from a much wider range of assessment initiatives that are occurring, although we can counter this possible criticism with many accounts of positive developments in pupil assessment in other sectors of education, and in other schools and LEAs. For example, we have said very little directly about assessment in primary schools, although we are aware of equally promising work in such schools (Ryan, 1988; Murphy, 1987b) which is comparable to the profiling work in secondary schools reviewed in Chapter 3.

It is our view that the face of educational assessment is changing through many of these initiatives. Many of them have managed to break away from the straightjacketed psychometric assumptions of traditional assessment in secondary schools. They have been at least as concerned, if not more so, with promoting good education through assessment, by ensuring that assessment facilitates the curriculum and teaching approaches being followed rather than cutting across them. Some would argue that this has been to the detriment of safeguarding standardized, so-called 'objective' testing procedures. The results may, on the psychometric model, be slightly less reliable as a result, although only in the strict sense of them being less easy to reproduce again in other circumstances.

Our own predominant concern is not for assessments to be psychometrically pure and reliable, but for them to play a constructive role in the educational process and as a part of that role to provide valid information about educational achievement in the fullest sense of the meaning of that phrase. Such achievement is not that which is *easily measurable,* but that which is *desirable* in terms of the broad aims of those concerned with what children gain from the process of education.

We see the greatest hope for such a change lying in the so-called 'alternative' assessment initiatives, on which we have concentrated most of our attention, particularly in Chapters 3–5. The attempt to reform public examinations has been a long drawn-out affair, and there is widespread feeling among many who have intimately been involved in this that little real progress has been made in terms of radically improving the deadening influence that examinations have had on schooling in this country (Macintosh, 1986; Nuttall, 1987a).

The fact that public examinations are not fulfilling the major need that there is for a constructive assessment system is widely acknowledged, for example in publications from the DES itself:

> it is widely recognised that, in its broader sense, assessment by public examinations can have two positive purposes – diagnosis and recording – the one analysing pupils' performance and identifying weaknesses in order to remedy them, the other recognising achievements attained. Both purposes can help motivate pupils to achieve more and attain a higher level of performance.... The question is how the public examination system can be made more effective as a measuring instrument. (DES, 1986, p.39)

The problem as ever is whether further attempts to improve the 'measuring instruments' used in public examinations will actually solve the problem. The boards have over a period of years devoted a vast amount of resources to this type of improvement, but despite all of the changes that have been made in terms of the introduction of more sophisticated and precise schemes of assessment, marking and grade awarding procedures, many of the core deficiencies have remained.

In 1969, Connaughton set out to review the whole issue of the validity of public examinations, and provided a comprehensive account of all of the problems associated with constructing the ideal form of assessment instrument. Many of the points he made had concerned Hartog and Rhodes (1935) a further 30 years before, and remain as insoluble problems, which need to be accepted as such if one is to stick with a formal public examination model (Mortimore and Mortimore, 1984). The dilemma is over whether it is worth going on and on trying to improve a system that is as fine-tuned as it ever will be to its particular, summative, purpose (though there will always be new issues to encompass within the model, e.g. gender and cultural bias). Certainly virtually everything that could be tried has been tried, to improve for example the reliability of public examinations, and in a limited way their validity as well. There is of course still the inevitable quandary involving a range of different groups wishing to use the results for a range of different purposes (Connaughton, 1969; Nuttall, 1987b), and the major selection function continues to dominate, although more recently this has been rivalled to some extent by the perceived effectiveness of public examinations as a mechanism for controlling the curriculum that is taught in schools around the country.

Connaughton's hope that further development work could improve the many shortcomings he found with the system must by now be wearing rather thin:

> If the boards (and of course teachers) could co-operate in this way in the exploration and specification of the role of examinations in curriculum development and evaluation, then, in the *not-too-distant future,* the criteria of a good examination procedure . . . may be fulfilled, with consequent benefit to the children being educated in our secondary schools. (Connaughton, 1969, p.176, our emphasis)

Part of the problem is that in the intervening 20 years teachers and examiners have still not come to terms with designing and operating a system of pupil assessment that is not hinged immutably to the end of secondary schooling, but rather can feed the processes of diagnosis, evaluation and guidance throughout each individual's experience of education. It may be that such a system, perhaps in the form of pupil profiling, will be brought in to complement public examinations, or in the course of time to replace them. However, the dangers of a dual system of assessment are already well understood and the existence of GCSE may make it hard for any other assessment initiative to gain any real credibility. This is certainly the prediction of one of those closely associated with the current profiling and records of achievement developments:

> Sadly, it seems more likely that the appeal of the existing examination tradition will prove vastly superior to that of a novel and relatively untried procedure. If this does indeed prove to be the case, one of the most significant outcomes of

the GCSE is likely to be the limitations it imposes on the parallel development of records of achievement. (Broadfoot, 1987, p.179)

This is a view, which has already been endorsed by Henry Macintosh in Chapter 5.

6.2 Ideals to be attained

A major challenge for those attempting to explore new initiatives in educational assessment, is the need to resist the powerful traditions and influences to which we have referred. A broader concept of educational achievement must certainly imply a broader range of assessment methods. This follows from the fact that many of the aspects of achievement that we now wish to assess cannot be assessed by formal written tests or examinations. In the same way that educational researchers have had to argue the case for alternative qualitative and interpretative research methods in order to improve the overall quality of research data, so increased status and kudos will have to be given to teachers who become actively involved in the collection and recording of qualitative, naturalistic, observational data on the achievements of their pupils (cf. Bridges *et al.* 1986). This is just one consequence of changed ideas about desirable characteristics for current assessment initiatives.

A review (Murphy and Pennycuick, 1985) of a range of recent educational reports and policy statements has revealed a high level of agreement in terms of the characteristics that ideally ought to be associated with improved assessment systems. They should thus,

1   record information about a much wider range of the achievements of pupils than have been emphasised through a narrow approach to educational assessment in the past;
2   lead to meaningful and positive descriptions of what all pupils can do;
3   promote rather than inhibit curriculum development and reform;
4   enhance pupil motivation and teacher morale and thus lead to an overall improvement in educational standards;
5   lead to a more harmonious relationship between assessment methods, curriculum design and teaching methods within individual schools. (Murphy and Pennycuick, 1985, p.2)

The assessment initiatives that we have given special attention to in this book have in many ways made considerable progress towards meeting these ideals. Of course there are problems – educational as well as logistical and organizational. Profiles, for example, could become overly-focused on the personal and the social (in large part because they will probably have to co-exist with GCSE) raising issues of surveillance and social control rather than the diagnosis of learning difficulties and the promotion of learning. Equally, graded tests and modular credit systems could lead to a very fragmented and test-dominated curriculum. Issues of coherence and of the pace and sequence of learning are crucial here, as is the capacity of the school, and more particularly the individual pupil, to generate an overview of what has been and can be achieved. Yet such problems are by no means insurmountable given the will to focus innovation and resources on the classroom in order to develop further our understanding and practice of the interrelation of teaching and assessment.

Unfortunately, at the current time, that political will seems to be lacking and the initiatives we have reviewed are likely to be overshadowed by GCSE. It may yet be the case however that the rise in proposals for modular courses, particularly within TVEI extension work may do something to force a reconsideration of the structure and rule systems that have been created around the initial wave of GCSE examinations. A lot depends on the ordering and reordering of political and educational interests outlined in Chapter 2. GCSE as it now exists measures up very poorly to our checklist of ideal characteristics (Murphy and Pennycuick, 1986; Murphy, 1988a), certainly falling down on the first three points and in many schools and curriculum areas the other two as well.

The year of 1988 may well be a crucial one in determining the direction of future developments in this respect. Apart from being the first year of the GCSE examinations, it is also to be the year in which a further DES policy statement on records of achievement is expected. This should lay down criteria for a system through which every school leaver in every secondary school will from 1990 receive a full and detailed record of his or her achievements. On top of all that it now seems that it will also be the year in which the foundations will be laid for a system of national tests at 7 (or thereabouts), 11 and 14, which it is proposed will be lined up alongside GCSE (at 16) as major indicators of the extent to which pupils, teachers, schools and LEAs reach the attainment targets which are to be legislated for and worked out on the basis of the *National Curriculum 5–6 Consultation Document* (DES, 1987b).

The assessment proposals contained within this consultation document are even further removed than GCSE from the ideals we have outlined for improved assessment systems, but because they are likely to dominate much of the debate about assessment changes in the next few years we will now consider how they relate to the issues raised in this book so far.

6.3 The national curriculum proposals for tests at 7, 11 and 14

During the months preceding the publication of the *National Curriculum 5–16 Consultation Document* (DES, 1987b) the Secretary of State for Education, Kenneth Baker, made a number of references to a system of national assessments that was to be introduced along with the national curriculum. This system of assessment, which at that stage was referred to as a system of 'benchmark tests' was to be based, we were told, on tests that 'would be set and marked by teachers but moderated externally' and these tests 'would be based on clear and challenging attainment targets for the key ages of 7, 11 and 14' (*The Times Educational Supplement,* 10 April 1987).

There was a good deal of concern (Murphy, 1987c) about these early announcements, which in many respects appeared rather puzzling in terms of:

1 The intended nature of these benchmark tests.
2 The purpose of the tests.
3 The extent to which teachers would actually become involved in setting and marking the tests.
4 The extent to which the attainment targets would represent the whole rather than selected parts of the national curriculum.
5 The likely impact on teaching that the tests would have in terms of narrowing teaching to a very great extent towards the 'attainment targets'.
6 The wisdom of linking attainment targets to specific ages, when it is widely recognized that pupils reach different levels of attainment at very different ages.
7 The resources that would be available for developing assessments that could actually perform the ambitious task being expected of them, for training teachers to carry out the assessments and for organizing the expensive process of moderating teachers' assessments in all schools throughout the country.

At the time of writing many of these issues remain unresolved. Perhaps most worrying of all is the continued lack of clarity, despite the publication of the *Consultation Document* and the further letter of 'Guidance for Curriculum Working Groups' in science and mathematics from Kenneth Baker (dated 24 August 1987), about the purpose of the tests (Murphy, 1988b). Even the GCSE examining groups, who on the basis of the consultation document proposals stand to gain a substantial increase in revenue through administering and moderating all of the tests for all of the age groups, are concerned. They have sought urgent clarification from the DES over this issue in the light of statements from ministers that the tests would on the one hand be used to diagnose specific learning difficulties in individuals and on the other would be used as a measure of the performances of teachers, schools and local education authorities. It would seem from all of this that once again assessments, which can usually only be designed specifically for one purpose, are likely to be used for any manner of other purposes – in most cases quite inappropriately (Nuttall, 1987b).

Another major irony in the *Consultation Document* (DES, 1987b) is in terms of the emphasis that it places on the fact that the proposed testing programme, aligned to specific attainment targets, is a 'proven and essential way towards raising standards of achievement' (DES, 1987b, p.10). There has been much conjecture (e.g. Wood, 1987; Howson, 1987) about where the origins of this proof lies. Much of the evidence from other countries (see Cohen, 1987, reviewed in Chapter 1) suggests that attainment targets when designed for a whole population of school pupils of a given age, are more likely to decrease expectations, have a harmful restricting influence on teaching approaches, and generally lower educational standards rather than raise them. This philosophy of raising performance through regular testing also contrasts markedly with an alternative philosophy, exposed in the much heralded Cockcroft Report (DES, 1982b), which has been reiterated in subsequent DES publications (e.g. DES, 1986) that 'No-one has ever grown taller as a result of being measured' (DES, 1982b, p.123).

Good systems of educational assessment, for example those meeting the ideals set out in Section 6.2, will undoubtedly have every chance of raising educational standards. However there is nothing to guarantee that 'regular testing' of whatever kind will necessarily improve standards. Sadly the evidence that we have from so many inappropriate and ill-conceived programmes of educational assessment is exactly the opposite of this.

A final issue that we will raise in relation to the national curriculum testing proposals is the role of teachers in the assessment process. This is a central theme, which we have returned to many times in this book, and which we will consider still further in the remainder of this chapter. It is our contention that much is to be gained from teachers having a central role in the assessment of their own pupils. The further in this direction that valid and credible systems of assessment can be taken, then the greater will be the chance of attaining the ideals set out in Section 6.2 of this chapter. On the other hand, the longer emphasis is placed on external systems of assessment, divorced and remote from schools, classrooms and teachers, the longer will the unhelpful divide between teaching, learning and assessment be perpetuated.

If there has been a U-turn in the national curriculum testing proposals it could well have been in relation to this very issue. In the early announcements, as we have already stated, the tests were to 'be set and marked by teachers but moderated externally' (*The Times Educational Supplement, 10 April 1987*). By the time the consultation document came out in August 1987, this had changed significantly to:

> The Secretaries of State envisage that much of the assessment at ages 7 (or thereabouts), 11 and 14, and at 16 in non-examined subjects, will be done by teachers as an integral part of normal classroom work. *But at the heart of the assessment process there will be nationally prescribed tests done by all pupils* to supplement the individual teachers' assessments. (DES, 1987b, p.11, our emphasis)

This statement when linked to the prominent role given to the DES's Assessment of Performance Unit 'in helping to steer the development and piloting of assessment instruments' (DES, 1987b, p.30) and to the GCSE examining groups in administering and moderating the system:

> The Secretaries of State hope that the moderation of teachers' assessments and whatever arrangements are needed for administering nationally set tests will be undertaken by the five GCSE examining groups, under contract from the School Examination and Assessment Council. (DES, 1987b, p.12)

can lead one to a quite different view about the nature of the role teachers will actually perform in the proposed system.

Altogether the proposals as set out in the consultation document run almost without exception in a direction that is contrary to the one advocated in this book. It may not be too late to rectify some of the worst aspects of these proposals, indeed as they stand they are almost certainly unworkable, so some changes will have to be made. However, the extent to which real modification can be accomplished, moving the proposed system, for example, away from age-related attainment targets and a system dominated by externally-devised tests of narrow measurable features of the national curriculum, remains to be seen.

6.4 What future for school-based assessment and evaluation?

What then of the future for the ideas, and indeed the specific practices, which we have been concerned to explore throughout this book? In essence these comprise the integral role of teacher and pupil in planning and using assessment in the process of teaching and learning, and the integration of assessment with formative school-based evaluation.

Clearly teacher involvement in the assessment process is a prerequisite for the realization of such ideas and to some extent at least this involvement seems likely to continue. In the uncertain relationship between the development of educational thinking and the development of political rhetoric about education, outlined in Chapter 2, the ideas of 'criterion-referencing' and 'diagnosis' seem to have emerged as crucially important. They will mean different things to different people and we must beware of a tightly-controlled and hierarchically-organized form of 'line management' emerging in the context of appraisal and accountability. Defining objectives and then designing overly mechanistic curriculum packages to 'deliver' them and tests to measure the effectiveness of delivery has been widely criticized in the United States and it would be foolish to repeat such mistakes here (Atkin, 1979; House, 1980). More positively, however, discussions of criterion-referencing signify a focus on the utility of assessment which takes us beyond the traditional, summative, selective function and closer to the formative school-based process. Similarly, as noted in Chapter 2, the interest in reporting what pupils 'know, understand and can do' (DES, 1985, p.2) must inevitably draw teachers more and more into assessment procedures since they are in the best position to make judgements of understanding and application; to test those 'aspects of attainment which may not easily or adequately be tested by [final] papers' (SEC, 1985, p.2).

A certain latitude exists then, a certain legitimating rhetoric from which it will be hard for policy-makers to retreat, but which of itself may not lead to significant change. Thus, for example, the spread of teacher-assessed elements in GCSE ought to bring some greater flexibility to the system in as much as far greater numbers of teachers will be involved in assessing their pupils' work and a good deal of this activity will revolve around practical work and fieldwork on one sort or another. Teachers ought to be in a better position both to assist their pupils in the learning process and to reflect on the quality and success (or lack of it) of the particular tasks they set and learning strategies they employ. However, as we have already noted in Chapter 1, current problems over pay and morale are bound to have an impact on the commitment and energy which teachers bring to the task of school-based assessment and evaluation, while opportunities for significant change are in any case limited by the National Criteria.

A great deal will depend on the initial pattern of teacher involvement which may solidify eventually into routine practice. It will also be important whether the dominant perception of GCSE remains as essentially that of an 'examination' with teacher involvement construed as one part of an overall, end-of-course, aggregatory judgement, rather than as an opportunity to provide pupils with feedback on their problems and achievements. GCSE, if developed sensibly, could provide an opportunity to broaden the *design* of assessment tasks not just the procedures for grading. Broadening the scope and nature of assessment tasks would involve a fundamental rethink of the role of assessment in GCSE on the part of teachers and examination boards alike. Essentially, it would involve regarding coursework assessment as an integral part of a learning-through-doing pedagogy, rather than simply the opportunity to ascertain (albeit through new techniques and in a more real and relevant context) what has-been-learned (Torrance, 1986c).

A crucial issue in this respect is moderation. A flexible and responsive approach to moderation could maximize the opportunity for teachers to experiment with different sorts of coursework assignments and gain experience of reflecting on the overall quality and effectiveness of their syllabus and teaching methods. This would involve the GCSE Examining Groups in making the most of the experience of consensus and inspection (as opposed to statistical) moderation which most of the CSE boards and some sections of the GCE boards have already had. They will also need to be prepared to argue with the Secondary Examinations Council and its successor for broader discussion of assessment objectives and marking criteria on the grounds of both the validity of the resulting grades and the professional development of teachers. If all of this happens then a more flexible model of moderation might yet emerge for the system as a whole than that currently envisaged by the GCSE General Criteria (cf. DES, 1985, p. 91). Such a model would place as much emphasis, if not more, on developing teachers' assessment skills and on the relationship between assessment, curriculum and pedagogy, as on the ever more extensive but ultimately unproductive task of monitoring marks and grades. This would involve Examining Groups liaising with local education authorities over in-service provision and specifically over the setting up and funding of local consortia of teachers and networks of visiting moderators. In this they could perhaps make use of networks already established through the later phases of the GCSE in-service training, supporting them through the new Grant Related In-Service Training (GRIST) funding arrangements. The key features for moderation procedures would be the maintenance of *regular* and *continuing* contacts with schools and between schools, throughout the duration of GCSE courses, rather than merely sampling and in effect remarking coursework products as a one-off exercise at the end of the course. A continuing dialogue about curriculum and teaching methods could then ensue with the emphasis placed as much on the *setting* of coursework assignments, as on the marking of them. Experienced departments already engaging in in-school evaluation and curriculum development would have a mechanism by which soundly-based argument and negotiation would have a place in moderation. Likewise, less experienced teachers in need of continuing support rather than end-of-course inspection could hope to build up this confidence rather than have it destroyed through the worst kind of statistical moderation (Murphy, 1982).

A similar scenario can be sketched out for the proposed 'benchmark tests'. A curriculum and its attendant scheme of assessment which is designed at considerable remove from the classroom and imposed in an even more hierarchical fashion than GCSE is likely to deskill teachers, lead to a narrowing of teaching methods and a lowering of educational standards. It would also be extremely expensive to construct, and implement, even supposing that the endeavour is restricted to assessing cohorts of pupils by paper and pencil tests. In fact recent work by the Assessment of Performance Unit Science team (much quoted by the DES as a source of expertise) and similar research developments in other curriculum areas suggests that small groups and individuals need to be focused on, with testing done orally, and in practical situations, if results are to be as valid and helpful as possible (Denvir and Brown, 1987; Gamble *et al.* 1984; Harlen, 1985). Thus, if the relationship of raising educational standards to the quality and pattern of assessment procedures is to be taken seriously, rather than merely being used as an excuse to pursue central control of the curriculum, money would be far better spent not on duplicating and supplying tests (from the APU or elsewhere) but on disseminating the overall findings and general implications of the work of the APU and other researchers much more widely, in order to encourage teachers to think more clearly about what it is they are trying to achieve and how they should go about trying to achieve it.

A pertinent point of contact between research and practice in the field of assessment is found in the issue of the pacing and sequencing of learning which many researchers have grappled with in relation to diagnosing learning problems and which teachers must grapple with in relation to classroom management and the practical decisions which must be taken about pupil progress. It is crucial that teachers have the opportunity to reflect on problems of diagnosing learning difficulties in the context of their own particular classrooms and be able to relate research to their own assessment practices. It is likely that many of the routine assessment practices of teachers would be found to be in need of improvement as a result of such a programme of in-service provision, but to reiterate the point about moderation in GCSE, encouraging teachers to develop and improve techniques and procedures within the classroom, and to work collaboratively to do this, is likely to be a far more effective way of raising educational standards in the longer term than a mammoth programme of testing and monitoring.

Such advocacy on our part may appear to slip into a 'teacher-knows-best' mode of thought, and so be at odds with current political thinking, and indeed with much public concern at the quality of the education service. This is not our intention. The wider community has as much right as teachers to take part in the broader curriculum debate, if not more, but the school-community relationship must involve dialogue, rather than prescription, if it is to be understood and effectively implemented by all parties; and certainly teachers, while not 'knowing best' *per se*, are in the best position 'to-come-to-know' what ought to be done with respect to general curricular concerns and particular pupil problems. In this they require, however, not only dialogue with the community, but also a broad framework of professional support to facilitate development and meet the sorts of in-service needs that we have outlined above.

It is for these reasons that, notwithstanding our recognition of the many problems, we suggest some form of modularization of the curriculum, combined with recording of achievement in the broadest sense, as the most appropriate focus for an alternative approach to improving the quality of teaching, learning and assessment in our schools. Modularization ought to attend to the need for both explicit curriculum planning and responsiveness to pupil need – setting out clearly and coherently what the intentions and content of a particular unit of work are while leaving it to the pupils, in dialogue with other adults including their teachers, to decide which 'building blocks' are most pertinent to their aptitudes and interests. Recording achievement – profiling – ought to encourage teachers to reflect on when, how and why they assess pupils' work, as well as providing the framework for LEA-based in-service work on the validity and comparability of the final Record. It should similarly encourage community, and especially parental, involvement in the processes of teaching and learning leading up to the production of a final Record, as well as community oversight of the validity and utility of whatever kind of final document emerges. Both modularization and recording achievement place teachers at the heart of the process of curriculum development and assessment, but as argued above this need not involve a paramount emphasis being placed on the autonomy of the teacher. While school-based curriculum development and assessment have increasingly come to be seen as a way in which teachers can avoid the legitimate scrutiny of their work we would argue that the reverse could be and should be the case with school-based dialogue between teachers and parents about curriculum and assessment, providing the most appropriate and legitimate forum for curriculum development and school evaluation. Turning this idea into a practical endeavour is an aspiration underpinning a number of pilot Record of Achievement schemes around the country. It has to be admitted that it is an endeavour which is still in its infancy. Furthermore, retaining sight of it while at the same time struggling to accommodate and ameliorate some of the other aspects of the National Curriculum proposals would represent an immense challenge to LEA officers and advisers, exam board personnel, and teachers. But it is a challenge which all of us working in education need to be prepared to engage in if many more generations of children are not to be condemned to the immensely limited and limiting vision of assessment which still pervades much policy and practice, and which is more in tune with the attitudes and aspirations of the nineteenth century, than the twenty-first.

Bibliography

Atkin, M.J. (1979). 'Educational accountability in the United States' *Educational Analysis* **1**, 5–21.

Ball, S. (1981). *Beachside Comprehensive*. Cambridge, Cambridge University Press.

Balogh, J. (1982). *Profile Reports for School Leavers*. York, Longman for Schools Council.

Beloe Report (1960). *Secondary School Examinations other than the GCEs* (Secondary School Examinations Council). London, HMSO.

Bloom, B.S. (1974). 'An introduction to mastery learning theory'. In Block, J.H. (ed.), *Schools, Society and Mastery Learning*. New York, Holt, Rinehart and Winston.

Bloom, B.S. (1976). *Human Characteristics and School Learning*. New York, McGraw-Hill.

Board of Education (1943). *Curriculum and Examinations in Secondary Schools* (The Norwood Report). London, HMSO.

Bowe, R. and Whitty, G. (1984). 'Teachers, boards and standards: the attack on school-based assessment in English public examinations at 16+'. In Broadfoot, P. (ed.), *Selection, Certification and Control*. London, Falmer Press.

Bowring, M. (1983). *Pupil Profile Development in Schools*. Hereford and Worcester Education and Industry Centre.

Bridges, D., Elliott, J. and Klass, C. (1986). 'Performance appraisal and naturalistic inquiry'. *Cambridge Journal of Education* **16** (3), 221–33.

Broadfoot, P. (1979). *Assessment, Schools and Society*. London, Methuen.

Broadfoot, P. (1981). 'What price classroom autonomy: two cautionary tales'. Paper presented at the 7th Annual BERA

Conference, Crewe and Alsager College, September 1981.

Broadfoot, P. (ed.) (1984a). *Selection, Certification and Control.* London, Falmer Press.

Broadfoot, P. (1984b). 'Profiling and the affective curriculum'. Paper presented at the Sociology of Education Conference, St. Hilda's College, Oxford, September 1984.

Broadfoot, P. (1986a). 'Assessment policy and inequality: the United Kingdom experience'. *British Journal of Sociology of Education* **7**(2), 205–24.

Broadfoot, P. (ed.) (1986b). *Profiles and Records of Achievement.* London, Holt, Rinehart and Winston.

Broadfoot, P. (1987). 'Records of achievement and the GCSE'. In Horton, T. (ed.), *GCSE: Examining the New System.* London, Harper and Row.

Brown, M. (1983). 'Graded tests in mathematics: the implications of various models for the mathematics curriculum'. Paper presented at the 9th Annual BERA Conference, London, September 1983.

Burgess, R. (1984). *Experiencing Comprehensive Education.* London, Methuen.

Burgess, T. and Adams, E. (eds) (1980). *Outcomes of Education.* Basingstoke, Macmillan.

Centre for Contemporary Cultural Studies (1981). *Unpopular Education.* London, Hutchinson.

Cohen, D. (1987). 'Evaluating standards: is there a way?' mimeo, MacQuarrie University, Australia.

Connaughton, I.M. (1969). 'The validity of examinations at 16–plus'. *Educational Review* **11**, 163–78.

Cox, C. and Boyson, R. (eds) (1975). *Black Paper 1975: The Fight for Education.* London, Dent.

Cox, C. and Dyson, A. (eds) (1971). *The Black Papers on Education.* London, Davis-Poynton.

Crowther Report (1959). *Report to the Minister of Education's Central Advisory Council: "15 to 18".* London, HMSO.

Denvir, B. and Brown, M. (1987). 'The feasibility of class administered diagnostic assessment in primary mathematics. *Educational Research* **29**, 2, 95–107.

Department of Education and Science (1977). *Education in Schools: A Consultative Document.* London, HMSO.

Department of Education and Science (1979). *Aspects of Secondary Education.* London, HMSO.

Department of Education and Science (1981). *The School Curriculum.* London, HMSO.

Department of Education and Science (1982a). *17+ A New Qualification.* London, HMSO.

Department of Education and Science (1982b). *Mathematics Counts.*

Report of the Committee of Inquiry into the Teaching of Mathematics in Schools (The Cockcroft Report). London, HMSO.

Department of Education and Science (1984). *Records of Achievement: A Statement of Policy*. London, HMSO.

Department of Education and Science (1985). *General Certificate of Secondary Education. The National Criteria. General Criteria*. London, HMSO.

Department of Education and Science (1986). *Better Schools. Evaluation and Appraisal Conference*. London, HMSO.

Department of Education and Science (1987a). *Records of Achievement: an Interim Report*. London, HMSO.

Department of Education and Science (1987b). *The National Curriculum 5–16. A Consultation Document*. London, HMSO.

Duffy, M.N. (1980). 'A logbook of personal achievement'. *Education* **155** (5), 119–20.

Elliott, J. and MacDonald, B. (eds) (1975). *People in Classrooms*. CARE Occasional Publications No. 2. Norwich, Centre for Applied Research in Education.

Ellis, T., Haddow, B., McWhirter, J. and McColgan, D. (1976). *William Tyndale The Teachers' Story*. London, Writers and Readers Publishing Cooperative.

Evans, J. (1985). *Teaching in Transition*. Milton Keynes, Open University Press.

Fairbairn, D.J. (1987). 'Pupil profiling: some policy issues from school-based practice'. *Journal of Education Policy* **2**(3), 223–34.

Further Education Unit (1979). *A Basis for Choice*. London, Further Education Unit.

Gagné, R.M. (1968). 'Learning hierarchies'. *Educational Psychologist* **6**, 1–9.

Gamble, R., Davey, A., Gott, R. and Welford, G. (1984). *Science at Age 15* APU Science Report for Teachers: 5, Hatfield, Association for Science Education.

Gipps, C. (ed.) (1986). *The GCSE: An Uncommon Examination*. Bedford Way Papers No. 29. London, Institute of Education.

Gipps, C. (1987). 'Differentiation in the GCSE'. *Forum* **29**(3), 76–8.

Goacher, B. (1983). *Recording Achievement at 16+*. York, Longman for Schools Council.

Goacher, B. (1984). *Selection Post–16: the Role of Examination Results*. Schools Council Examinations Bulletin 45. London, Methuen.

Goldstein, H. (1986). 'Models for equating test scores and for studying the comparability of public examinations'. In Nuttall, D. (ed.), *Assessing Educational Achievement*. London, Falmer Press.

Goldstein, H. and Blinkhorn, S. (1977). 'Monitoring educational standards: an inappropriate model'. *Bulletin of the British*

Psychological Society **30**, 309–11.

Goldstein, H. and Nuttall, D. (1986). 'Can graded assessments, records of achievement and modular assessment co-exist with the GCSE?' In Gipps, C.V. (ed.), *The GCSE: An Uncommon Examination*. Bedford Way Papers No. 29. London, Institute of Education.

Goodson, I. (1983). *School Subjects and Curriculum Change*. London, Croom Helm.

Gretton, J. and Jackson, M. (1976). *William Tyndale*. London, George Allen and Unwin.

Hamilton, D. (1980). 'Adam Smith and the moral economy of the classroom system'. *Journal of Curriculum Studies* **12**(4), 281–98.

Hamilton, D., Jenkins, D., King, C., MacDonald, B. and Parlett, M. (eds) (1977). *Beyond the Numbers Game*. London, Macmillan.

Hammersley, M. and Hargreaves, A. (eds) (1983). *Curriculum Practice*. London, Falmer Press.

Hammersley, M. and Scarth, J. (1986). *The Impact of Examinations on Secondary School Teaching*. School of Education Research Report. Milton Keynes, Open University.

Harding, A., Page, B. and Rowell, S. (1980). *Graded Objectives in Modern Languages*. London, Centre for Information on Language Teaching and Research (CILT).

Hargreaves, A. (1988). 'The crisis in motivation and assessment'. In Hargreaves, A. and Reynolds, D. (eds). *Educational Policy Initiatives*. London, Falmer Press.

Hargreaves, D. (1982). *The Challenge for the Comprehensive School*. London, Routledge and Kegan Paul.

Harlen, W. (ed.) (1985). *Science in Schools Age 11: Report No. 4*. London, DES.

Harrison, A. (1982). *Review of Graded Tests*. Schools Council Examinations Bulletin 41. London, Methuen Educational.

Harrison, A. (1985). 'Graded assessment'. In *E206 Block 4 Supplementary Reading*. Milton Keynes, Open University.

Hartog, P. and Rhodes, E. (eds) (1935). *An Examination of Examinations*. London, Macmillan.

Hirst, P. and Peters, R. (1970). *The Logic of Education*. London, Routledge and Kegan Paul.

Hitchcock, G. (1986). 'Instituting profiling within a school'. In Broadfoot, P. (ed.), *Profiles and Records of Achievement*. London, Holt, Rinehart and Winston.

Holt, J. (1969). *The Underachieving School*. London, Pitman.

Horton, T. (ed.) (1986). *GCSE: Examining the New System*. London, Harper and Row.

House, E.R. (1980). *Evaluating with Validity*, Beverly Hills, Sage Publications.

Howson, G. (1987). 'The quest for standards'. *The Times Educational*

Supplement 16 October 1987.

Inner London Education Authority (1984). *Improving Secondary Schools*. London, ILEA.

Joint Board for Pre-vocational Education (1984). *The Certificate of Pre-vocational Education, Consultative Documenty*. London, B/TEC and City and Guilds of London Institute.

Jones, K. (1983). *Beyond Progressive Education*. Basingstoke, Macmillan.

Lawton, D. (1975). *Class, Culture and the Curriculum*. London, Routledge and Kegan Paul.

Levy, P. and Goldstein, H. (1984). *Tests in Education: A Book of Critical Reviews*. London, Academic Press.

MacDonald, B. (1979). 'Hard times – accountability in England'. *Educational Analysis* **1**(1), 23–44.

MacDonald, B. and Walker, R. (1976). *Changing the Curriculum*. London, Open Books.

Macintosh, H. (1979). 'Schools Council project History 13–16: The CSE examination, some problems of assessment' *Teaching History* **24** and **25**, June and October.

Macintosh, H.G. (1982). 'The prospects for public examinations in England and Wales'. *Educational Analysis* **4**(3), 13–20.

Macintosh, H.G. (1985). 'The politics of examining'. *Secondary Heads Association Review* **79**(247), 935–45.

Macintosh, H.G. (1986). 'The prospects for public examinations in England and Wales.' In Nuttall, D. (1986b) *Assessing Educational Achievement* London, Falmer Press.

Macintosh, H.G. and Hale, D.E. (1976). *Assessment and the Secondary School Teacher*. London, Routledge and Kegan Paul.

Ministry of Education (1963). *Half our future* (The Newsom Report). London, HMSO.

Morris, N. (1961). 'An historian's view of examinations.' In Wiseman, S. (ed.) *Examinations and English Education* Manchester, Manchester University Press.

Mortimore, J. and Mortimore, P. (1984). *Secondary School Examinations: The Helpful Servants, Not the Dominating Master*. Bedford Way Papers No. 18. London, Heinemann.

Murphy, R.J.L. (1982). 'Statistical moderation – a critique'. In *Combining Teacher Assessment with Examining Board Assessment*. Aldershot, Associated Examining Board.

Murphy, R.J.L. (1984). 'The impact of "examinations research" on policy and practice'. Paper presented at an Associated Examining Board Research Unit Seminar on 1 May 1984.

Murphy, R.J.L. (1986). 'The Emperor has no clothes: grade criteria and the GCSE'. In Gipps, G. (1986).

Murphy, R.J.L. (1987a). 'A changing role for examination boards?' In Horton, T. (ed.), *GCSE: Examining the New System*. London,

Harper and Row.

Murphy, R.J.L. (1987b). 'Pupil assessment in Primary Schools'. *Forum* Autumn 1987.

Murphy, R.J.L. (1987c). 'Assessing a National Curriculum'. *Journal of Education Policy* **2**(4), 317–23.

Murphy, R.J.L. (1988a). 'The birth of GCSE'. In Hargreaves, A. and Reynolds, D. (eds), *Educational Policy: Controversies and Critiques*. Lewes, Falmer Press.

Murphy, R.J.L. (1988b) 'Great Education Reform Bill for Testing. A Critique'. *Local Government Studies* 14(1), 39–45.

Murphy, R.J.L. and Pennycuick, D.B. (1985). 'Evaluating current initiatives in educational assessment: graded assessments and GCSE'. Paper presented to the Nuffield Assessment Seminar Group, London, November 1985.

Murphy, R.J.L. and Pennycuick, D.B. (1986). 'Graded assessment and the GCSE'. In Horton, T. (ed.), *GCSE: Examining the New System*. London, Harper and Row.

Newbould, C.A. and Massey, A.J. (1984). 'Initial survey of views on aspects of graded assessment'. Report for the Project on the Assessment of Graded Objectives, Midland Examining Group.

Nisbet, J. and Broadfoot, P. (1980). *The Impact of Research on Policy and Practice in Education*. Aberdeen, Aberdeen University Press.

Norton, B. (1979). 'Charles Spearman and the general factor of intelligence'. *Journal of the History of the Behavioural Sciences* **16**(15), 142–54.

Nuttall, D. (1971). *The 1968 CSE Monitoring Experiment*. Schools Council Working Paper 34. London, Evans/Methuen Educational.

Nuttall, D.L. (1975). 'Examinations in education'. In Cox, P.R., Miles, H.B. and Peel, J. (eds), *Equalities and Inequalities in Education*. London, Academic Press.

Nuttall, D.L. (1983). 'Monitoring in North America'. *Westminster Studies in Education* **6**, 63–90.

Nuttall, D. (1984). 'Doomsday or new dawn? The prospects for a common system of examining at 16+. In Broadfoot, P. (ed.), *Selection, Certification and Control*. London, Falmer Press.

Nuttall, D. (1986a). 'Problems in the measurement of change'. In Nuttall, D. (ed.), *Assessing Educational Achievement*. London, Falmer Press.

Nuttall, D. (ed.) (1986b). *Assessing Educational Achievement*. London, Falmer Press.

Nuttall, D.L. (1987a). 'The current assessment scene'. *Coombe Lodge Report* **19**(7), 375–92.

Nuttall, D.L. (1987b). 'Testing, testing, testing'. *Education Review* **1**, 2, 32–35.

Nuttall, D.L. and Goldstein, H. (1984). 'Profiles and graded tests: the technical issues'. In *Profiles in Action*. London, FEU.

Orr, L. and Nuttall, D. (1983). *Determining Standards in the Proposed Single System of Examining at 16+*. Comparability in Examinations. Occasional paper 2. London, Schools Council.

Oxford Delegacy of Local Examinations (1983). *OCEA Newsletter* Issue No. 1, April. Oxford, University of Oxford Delegacy of Local Examinations.

Oxford Delegacy of Local Examinations (1984). *The Story So Far. A Report from the OCEA Management Committee to the Delegates of Local Examinations*, May. Oxford, University of Oxford Delegacy of Local Examinations.

Pennycuick, D.B. (1985). 'What has Australia to offer the Graded Test Movement (and what has it to offer to Australia)?' *Westminster Studies in Education* **8**, 65–76.

Pennycuick, D.B. (1986). 'The development, use and impact of graded tests, with particular reference to modern languages, mathematics and science'. Unpublished Ph.D. thesis, Department of Education. Southampton, Southampton University.

Pennycuick, D.B. (1987). 'Issues in the implementation of graded testing'. In H.D. Black and W.B. Dockrell (eds). *New Developments in Educational Assessments*. BJEP Monograph No. 3. Edinburgh, Scottish Academic Press.

Pennycuick, D.B. and Murphy, R.J.L. (1986a). The impact of the graded test movement on classroom teaching and learning. *Studies in Educational Evaluation* **12**, 275–9.

Pennycuick, D.B. and Murphy, R.J.L. (1986b). 'Mastery, validity and comparability issues in relation to graded assessment schemes'. *Studies in Educational Evaluation* **12**, 305–11.

Pennycuick, D.B. and Murphy, R.J.L. (1988). *The Impact of Graded Tests*. Lewes, Falmer Press.

Pilliner, A. (1979). 'Norm-referenced and criterion-referenced tests–an evaluation'. In *Issues in Educational Assessment*. Edinburgh, Scottish Education Department.

Popham, W.J. (1978). *Criterion-referenced measurement*. Englewood Cliffs, NJ, Prentice-Hall.

Power, C. *et al.* (1982). *National Assessment in Australia. An Evaluation of the Australian Studies in Student Performance Project*. ERDC Report No. 35.

Radnor, H. (1987). *GCSE – The Impact of the Introduction of GCSE at LEA and School Level*. Slough, NFER.

Ranson, S. (1984). 'Towards a tertiary tripartism: new codes of social control and the 17+'. In Broadfoot, P. (ed.), *Selection, Certification and Control*. London, Falmer Press.

Ranson, S., Gray, J., Jesson, D., and Jones, B. (1986). 'Exams in context: values and power in educational accountability'. In

Nuttall, D. (ed.), *Assessing Educational Achievement*. London, Falmer Press.

Rutherford, W.L. (1979). 'Criterion-referenced programmes: the missing element'. *Journal of Curriculum Studies* **11**(1), 47–52.

Ryan, A.S. (1988). *Partnerships in Assessment. Pupil-centred Profiling in a Middle School*. Department of Education Occasional Publication. Southampton, Southampton University.

Salter, B. and Tapper, T. (1986). 'Department of Education and Science – steering a new course'. In Horton, T. (ed.), *GCSE: Examining the New System*. London, Harper and Row.

Scottish Council for Research in Education (1977). *Pupils in Profile*. Edinburgh, SCRE.

Scottish Council for Research in Education (1982). *Modules for All*. Edinburgh, SCRE.

Scottish Education Department (1969). *Pupils' Progress Records*. Edinburgh, HMSO.

Scottish Education Department (1977). *The Structure of the Curriculum in the Third and Fourth Years of Scottish Secondary Schools* (The Munn Report). Edinburgh, SED.

Scottish Vocational Preparation Unit (1982). *Assessment in Youth Training: Made to Measure?* Glasgow, Jordanhill College of Education.

Secondary Examinations Council (1985). *Coursework Assessment in GCSE*. London, SEC.

Spens Report (1938). *Report of the Consultative Committee on Secondary Education: With Special Reference to Grammar Schools and Technical High Schools*. London, HMSO.

Stake, R. (1967). 'The countenance of educational evaluation'. *Teachers' College Record* **68**, 523–40.

Stansbury, D. (1985). 'Assessment and recording'. Paper presented at the Records of Experience Conference, School of Education, University of Nottingham, 16 March.

Stenhouse, L. (1975). *An Introduction to Curriculum Research and Development*. London, Heinemann.

Stevens, A. (1987). 'Degrees of co-operation'. *Education* **169**(18), May.

Stevenson, M. (1983). 'Pupil profiles – an alternative to conventional examinations?' *British Journal of Educational Studies* **31**, 102–16.

Stronach, I. (1986). 'The new assessment'. Centre for Applied Research in Education. Norwich, University of East Anglia, mimeo.

Swales, T. (1979). *Record of Personal Achievement: an Independent Evaluation of the Swindon RPA Scheme*. Schools Council Pamphlet 16. London, Schools Council.

Times Educational Supplement (1982). *New Profiling Draws Heavy Criticism*,

19 February, p.12.

Times Educational Supplement (1987). *Tory Radicals Call for Return of O-Levels*, 15 May 1987, p.5.

Torrance, H. (1982). *Mode III Examining: Six Case Studies*. York, Longmans for the Schools Council.

Torrance, H. (1984). 'Teachers, pupils and exams'. In Schostak, J. and Logan, T. (eds), *Pupil Experience*. London, Croom Helm.

Torrance, H. (1985). *Case-studies in School-based Examining*. Department of Education Occasional Publication. Southampton, University of Southampton.

Torrance, H. (1986a). 'Assessment and examinations: social context and educational practice'. Ph.D. Thesis, Norwich, Centre for Applied Research in Education.

Torrance, H. (1986b). 'GCSE and control of the secondary curriculum'. *Curriculum* 7(2), 84–9.

Torrance, H. (1986c). 'School-based assessment in GCSE: aspirations, problems, and possibilities'. In Gipps, C. (ed.), *The GCSE: An Uncommon Examination*. Bedford Way Papers No. 29. London, Institute of Education.

Torrance, H. (1987). 'Differentiation and the role of the teacher'. *Forum* 29(3), 78–80.

Tyler, R. (1986). 'Changing concepts of educational evaluation'. *International Journal of Educational Research* 10(1), monograph.

Valentine, C. (1932). *The Reliability of Examinations*. London, University of London Press.

Vernon, P. (ed.) (1957). *Secondary School Selection*. London, Methuen.

Warwick, D. (1987). *The Modular Curriculum*. Oxford, Blackwell.

Whitty, G. (1976). 'Teachers and examiners'. In Whitty, G. and Young, M. (eds), *Explorations in the Politics of School Knowledge*. Driffield, Nafferton.

Whitty, G. (1983). 'Missing: a policy on the curriculum'. In Wolpe, A. and Donald, J. (eds), *Is There Anyone Here from Education?* London, Pluto Press.

Wilby, P. (1979). 'Towards a comprehensive curriculum'. In Pluckrose, H. and Wilby, P. (eds), *The Conditions of English Schooling*. Harmondsworth, Penguin.

Williams, N. (1986). 'The first ten years of examinations'. *Teaching History* 46, October.

Wilmott, A. (1986). 'The Oxford Certificate of Educational Achievement'. In Broadfoot, P. (ed.), *Profiles and Records of Achievement*. London, Holt, Rinehart and Winston.

Wilmott, A. and Nuttall, D. (1975). *The Reliability of Examinations at 16+*. London, Macmillan Educational.

Wood, R. (1978). 'Limitations of psychometric models and practices when applied to achievement tests'. Paper presented at an Associated Examining Board Research Unit Seminar,

28 April 1978.

Wood, R. (1982). 'Educational and psychological measurement: further efforts at differentiation'. *Educational Analysis* **4**(3), 119–34.

Wood, R. (1984). 'Observations on criterion referenced assessment'. Paper prepared for a seminar held at the Senior Secondary Assessment Board of Australia, 20 August 1984.

Wood, R. (1986). 'The agenda for educational measurement'. In Nuttall, D. (ed.), *Assessing Educational Achievement*. London, Falmer Press.

Wood, R. (1987). 'Voodoo Tests'. In *Times Educational Supplement*, 25 September 1987, 25.

Wright, N. (1977). *Progress in Education*. London, Croom Helm.

Yates, A. and Pidgeon, D. (1957). *Admission to Grammar Schools*. London, Newnes.

Young, M. (1971). 'An approach to the study of curricula as socially organised knowledge'. In Young, M. (ed.), *Knowledge and Control*. London, Collier Macmillan.

Index